WATSON V.
CENTURY TECHNOLOGIES, INC.

Second Edition

WATSON V.
CENTURY TECHNOLOGIES, INC.

Second Edition

Theresa D. Moore

Attorney at Law
University of California
Hastings College of the Law
Professor Adjunct

with

Patrick De Poy

Attorney at Law

TRIAL BY FIRE™ CASE SERIES
LEGAL ADVOCACY WITH NEW AND MODERN EVIDENCE

NATIONAL INSTITUTE FOR TRIAL ADVOCACY

Address inquiries to:

Reprint Permission
National Institute for Trial Advocacy
1685 38th Street, Suite 200
Boulder, CO 80301-2735
Phone: (800) 225-6482
Fax: (720) 890-7069
Email: permissions@nita.org

ISBN 978-1-60156-795-6
eISBN 978-1-60156-796-3

FBA 1795

Printed in the United States of America

CONTENTS

Juror Focus Group

Appendices

ACKNOWLEDGMENTS

Thank you to attorney Patrick DePoy for his stellar work on *Watson v. Century Technologies, Inc.* He has the instincts and the work ethic of a true trial lawyer. His energy, enthusiasm, and legal acumen are immeasurable, and it has been my honor to work with him.

Thank you to Ana Costa of Barkley Reporters for her graciousness and continual desire to aid in legal education, and for truly making it happen to enable us to include actual transcripts in modern format.

And, finally, thank you to Balinda Dunlop of Barkley Reporters for her tireless work in preparing *Watson v. Century Technologies, Inc.* transcripts after hours of reporting actual cases. Balinda has traveled all over the world working on cases of great import, and is one of the best reporters I have ever worked with in my legal career.

The National Institute for Trial Advocacy wishes to thank Facebook for its permission to use likenesses of its website as part of these teaching materials, as well as American Greetings for its permission to reproduce one of its greeting cards as an exhibit. Very special thanks go to Marty Cooper, who altered the course of human history in ways that couldn't be imagined in the 1970s, when he invented the first mobile cellular phone for Motorola. It was an honor to receive permission from the man himself to reproduce his photo in this case file.

Case Summary

Watson v. Century Technologies, Inc. is a civil action for employment discrimination. A businesswoman is suddenly fired, finding herself the odd woman out in an organization getting younger by the day.

Plaintiff Sharon Watson was a respected senior sales executive working in a technology-based sales company. Century Technologies, Inc. sells telecommunications equipment to businesses throughout the country, and Watson has been with the company since it started selling beepers over twenty-five years ago.

Danielle Khouri, the new face of Century and a rising star in the tech world, was brought in to shake things up. Sharon's exceptional career comes to an abrupt end when she is fired from her job.

A case of age discrimination, or a simple case of parties not seeing eye to eye on the future of a company? Either side can make a compelling case given the exhibits, testimony, and witnesses.

SPECIAL INSTRUCTIONS FOR USE AS A FULL TRIAL

All years in these materials are stated in the following form:

YR-0 indicates the actual year in which the case is being tried (i.e., the present year);

YR-1 indicates the preceding year (please use the actual year);

YR-2 indicates the next preceding year (please use the actual year); et cetera.

Any or all of the witnesses can be called by either party. Each party may call no more than four witnesses of their choice, including hostile witnesses. The expert witness is optional; the materials in this case file can be used effectively without the additional testimony of the expert witness.

The Federal Rules of Evidence apply.

The Local Rules for Mock Trials and Pretrial Conferences apply and are set forth in Appendix A.

The applicable law is contained in the statutes and proposed jury instructions set forth in Appendices B and C, respectively.

Electronic files for the exhibits are available for download here:

Website: http://bit.ly/1P20Jea
Password: Watson2

U.S. DISTRICT COURT
FOR THE STATE OF NITA
Civil Division

SHARON WATSON,	)	
	)	CAL: 2013-CIV-10886
Plaintiff,	)	**COMPLAINT FOR DAMAGES**
	)	**FOR AGE DISCRIMINATION IN**
v.	)	**EMPLOYMENT IN VIOLATION**
	)	**OF NITA CIVIL RIGHTS ACT**
CENTURY TECHNOLOGIES, INC.,	)	**775 NCS § 5/101** *et seq.*
	)	
	)	**DEMAND FOR JURY TRIAL**
Defendant.	)	

COMES NOW, Plaintiff Sharon Watson, by and through the undersigned counsel, and makes this Complaint against Defendant Century Technologies, Inc. (Century). In support thereof, Plaintiff states as follows:

PARTIES

1. Plaintiff is an individual who resides at the above-captioned address. At all relevant times herein, Plaintiff resided in Nita City, Nita.

2. Defendant Century is a corporation, authorized to do business in the State of Nita, which at all relevant times owned, controlled, and managed an information technology (IT) consulting firm.

JURISDICTION

3. This Court has diversity jurisdiction over this action pursuant to 22 Nita Code § 1332.

4. This Court has personal jurisdiction over Defendant Century pursuant to 22 Nita Code § 1332.

5. This Court is the proper venue for this matter pursuant to § 6-202(8) of the Courts and Judicial Proceedings Article of the Nita Code in that the cause of action which is the subject of this case arose in Nita City, Nita.

FACTUAL BACKGROUND

6. Between YR-25 and May 19, YR-2, Plaintiff Sharon Watson was an employee of Century, employed in various positions and capacities culminating in her promotion to the position of Assistant Vice President of Marketing.

7. Defendant Century is an IT consulting firm, and is in the business of selling and marketing computer products and software to other corporations and businesses. Century incorporated on or about March 18, YR-28.

8. Between January 1, YR-3, and her termination, Plaintiff experienced regular harassment, humiliation, and degradation as a result of her age.

9. Plaintiff lodged multiple complaints with other executives, including Danielle Khouri, regarding the derogatory comments, describing the behavior and treatment as unacceptable. The behavior continued until her eventual termination.

10. On May 19, YR-2, Khouri informed Plaintiff that she was terminated effective immediately. Khouri informed Plaintiff she would be given six months of severance pay and a continuation of her health care benefits for a calendar year. Khouri said she would not discuss the decision any further "on the advice of the lawyers."

11. Plaintiff has not been able to secure employment since her termination from Century.

COUNT ONE: AGE DISCRIMINATION

12. Plaintiff restates and realleges each and every allegation set forth above as if fully set forth herein.

13. Defendant Century's conduct as alleged above constitutes discrimination based on age in violation of the Nita Civil Rights Act (NCRA) of YR-17. *See* 775 NCS § 5/101 *et seq.* (YR-3).

14. At all times relevant to this complaint, Century was, and continues to qualify as, an employer under the NCRA. Century employs over 500 people throughout the United States, is incorporated under the laws of Nita, and has established its headquarters in Nita City, Nita.

15. At the time of her termination and at the time of Century's refusal to promote her, Plaintiff was over the age of forty and a member of a protected class as articulated by the NCRA.

16. Defendant Century engaged in unfavorable treatment, verbal harassment, and discriminatory conduct against Plaintiff because of her age, in whole or in part, in violation of the NCRA.

17. Defendant Century's agent, Danielle Khouri, terminated Plaintiff, in whole or in part, because of her age, despite her stellar performance as an executive.

18. Defendant is vicariously liable for the conduct of its agent, Danielle Khouri, and for the environment under which Plaintiff was made to suffer as a result of illegal age discrimination and harassment.

* * *

WHEREFORE, Plaintiff respectfully requests judgment against Defendant in an amount to be determined at a proceeding following trial, plus costs of suit, and such other and further relief as this Court deems just and proper.

Dated: February 1, YR-1

Respectfully Submitted,

Morgan Ellis

Morgan Ellis
Attorney for Plaintiff

JURY DEMAND

Plaintiff, by and through the undersigned counsel, hereby demands trial by jury of all issues in this matter.

Dated: February 1, YR-1

Respectfully Submitted,

Morgan Ellis

Morgan Ellis
Attorney for Plaintiff

U.S. DISTRICT COURT
FOR THE STATE OF NITA
Civil Division

SHARON WATSON,	)	
	)	
Plaintiff,	)	CAL: 2011-CIV-10886
v.	)	
	)	**ANSWER**
CENTURY TECHNOLOGIES, INC.,	)	
	)	
Defendant.	)	

COMES NOW Defendant, Century Technologies, Inc. ("Century"), by and through the undersigned counsel, and makes this Answer to Plaintiff Sharon Watson.

PARTIES

1. Defendant Century is without sufficient information to admit or deny the allegations in ¶ 1 and, therefore, demands strict proof thereof.

2. Admit.

JURISDICTION

3. The allegation in ¶ 3 states a legal conclusion as to which no response is required.

4. The allegation in ¶ 4 states a legal conclusion as to which no response is required.

5. The allegation in ¶ 5 states a legal conclusion as to which no response is required.

FACTUAL BACKGROUND AND CLAIM ONE

6. Defendant Century generally denies each and every allegation set forth in the unverified Complaint, and the whole thereof, and each and every cause of action alleged therein, and further expressly denies that as a direct or proximate cause of any acts or omissions on the part of the Defendant, Plaintiff sustained or suffered any injury or damages.

* * *

WHEREFORE, Defendant respectfully requests that the Court dismiss Plaintiff's claim, enter judgment in favor of Defendant Century, and award Defendant costs, attorney fees, and such other and further relief as the Court deems appropriate.

Dated: March 1, YR-1

Respectfully Submitted,

Chris Q. Dunne

Chris Q. Dunne
Attorney for Defendant

EXHIBITS

Exhibit 1

To: SASSOWER, Aaron
From: WATSON, Sharon
Date: February 21, YR-2
Subject: Mockery & Learning the Business

Aaron,

I wanted to follow up on our conversation earlier. I apologize for losing my cool a bit, but I think this bears repeating: I have been at this company for over twenty years, and the lack of respect you have shown me and some of the other veteran employees here is unacceptable.

I hope we can learn from each other. I know you joke about the dinosaurs and old geezers in this office who don't have **Facebook** yet, but we're trying to learn. Your degrading us doesn't help. And believe me, we see that you're a young pup with no sales experience. We'd like to help you see our side of the business while we try to learn yours.

I hope we can learn to work well together. But I have to say, if I see the kind of disrespect from you and some others in New Media that you've demonstrated in these trainings, I'm taking it back to Jim and Danielle.

Sharon

To: WATSON, Sharon
From: STANCIL, Jim
Date: July 12, YR-2
Subject: Re: Recent Incidents

Sharon, as your friend, I have to advise against that. You've seen how this company is changing these days. You've got a good job, you make good money, and you're not getting any younger—unlike this company. Can't we let sleeping dogs lie on this one? They're just kids goofing around. They don't mean anything by it. Come see me if you need to *before going to Danielle*.

Jim

To: STANCIL, James
From: WATSON, Sharon
Date: July 11, YR-2
Subject: Recent Incidents

Jim,

You have just gotta be kidding me with the comments from these kids. Asking us if we're still awake? Asking us if we need to take our Ensure or whatever the heck that little brat said today?

We go way back, Jim. Are you going to allow this? I mean, these changes are one thing; we all know the company's going in a new direction. But do I have to take these put-downs from Khouri's minions while I lead the company in sales?

I'm going to Danielle if I don't get the right answer from you.

To: BREDEMANN, Cynthia
From: KHOURI, Danielle
Date: June 21, YR-1
Subject: PR Nightmare

Thanks for all that, Cynthia!

We'll write it all up for a newsletter, or some kind of web promo. This Sharon thing is turning into a headache, so we'll probably leave your praise of Sharon out! Hahaha.

And, of course, you scratch our back, we'll scratch yours. Let me know when you need a hardware upgrade, and we'll see what we can do. Thanks for your help.

Danielle

To: KHOURI, Danielle
From: BREDEMANN, Cynthia
Date: June 26, YR-1
Subject: RE: PR Nightmare

Well, you know our business has been expanding over the last five years or so. We started on the road, but now we're dealing with storefronts and trying to plant our flag in neighborhoods around Nita City. You guys have been amazing, not just with the hardware but consulting on social media. So much of the business is getting your brand out there. Can't do that by giving my drivers beepers, right?

Hardware has been critical. We need mobile registers that accept credit cards, and your team came up with those for us. You set up all our computers in our storefronts, got our employees laptops and smartphones. You've been terrific on that front. Sharon actually was very helpful in getting us a discount on some things we needed.

Once we started our website and developed a social media presence, Sharon was useless. She said, "You're a smart young gal, you figure it out." (No wonder you fired her.) Luckily, you had other employees willing to help. Our website was booming, we had web orders, promotional deals were bringing people into our stores, people started following the trucks on Twitter. Just terrific stuff. The numbers speak for themselves. Here's a chart of our gross profits with the single truck and then once we teamed up with Century.

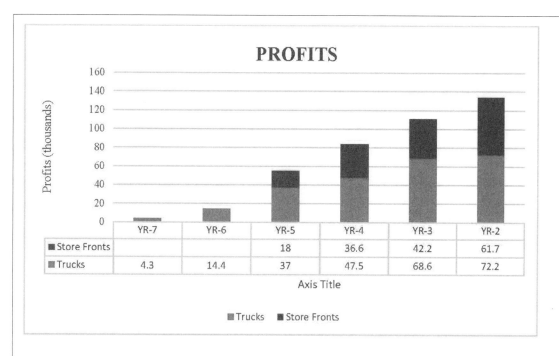

PROFITS

	YR-7	YR-6	YR-5	YR-4	YR-3	YR-2
■ Store Fronts			18	36.6	42.2	61.7
■ Trucks	4.3	14.4	37	47.5	68.6	72.2

Axis Title

■ Trucks   ■ Store Fronts

Of course, not all of this is because of you guys! Most of it is my amazing cooking and the hard work of my employees. But I think we're growing faster, and more consistently, thanks to you.

To: BREDEMANN, Cynthia
From: KHOURI, Danielle
Date: June 21, YR-1
Subject: PR Nightmare

Well, let's let you use your own words, and we'll write something up from that. How do you feel about the great new sales team at Century? How have we helped your business?

To: KHOURI, Danielle
From: BREDEMANN, Cynthia
Date: June 21, YR-1
Subject: RE: PR Nightmare

Danielle,

Glad to help out any way that I can. Between you and me, I am glad you're trimming the fat. Friends of mine say that Sharon and some of your more "experienced" employees are getting just awful and crotchety. I hate to be mean, but these were terrible sales people and just didn't understand business in the twenty-first century.

Are we talking a commercial? Radio promo? Some kind of web ad? A web ad would work best for me. I want to get something out of this, too. Also, what do you need me to say? I'll let you write the script, I'll say whatever you want.

Maybe we can talk discounts on my next order, too?

To: BREDEMANN, Cynthia
From: KHOURI, Danielle
Date: June 21, YR-1
Subject: PR Nightmare

Hi Cynthia,

As one of our favorite clients, I hope you know how much we appreciate your business during these somewhat challenging times. As a chef, you know that if you're making an omelette, you need to crack a few eggs! Tell that to the *Nita City Gazette* after they ran that ridiculous puff piece on Sharon Watson.

For us, it's a PR nightmare, and we've already lost a few clients. Any chance you'd be willing to do a promo with us? It'd be great cross-promotional synergy and would increase your web hits if we sell it right. Win-win. Interested?

Thanks,
Danielle

To: MCDERMOTT, Xavier
From: KHOURI, Danielle
Date: June 19, YR-1
Subject: Phone Conversation

Xavier,

Aaron meant no disrespect, and neither do I. We just want to keep your business. As a businessman yourself, you know that this is a numbers game and Sharon was not hitting hers. I know she's your best friend, but please don't break our relationship in the heat of the moment.

After all the yelling and screaming you did the other day, I can tell you're upset. Please think rationally before you break up this mutually beneficial relationship.

Best,
DK

To: KHOURI, Danielle
From: MCDERMOTT, Xavier
Date: June 18, YR-1
Subject: Phone Conversation

Danielle,

Based on our phone conversation earlier, I think it's only fair I let you know I don't expect us to continue using Century.

We pride ourselves on loyalty and treating people with decency. You and your new team treated Sharon and older members of your staff like dirt, and I simply can't abide by that. I've been doing business with Sharon and Century for twenty years, and never have I seen such rapid changes so quickly. You're alienating other clients, too. I'm a member of the business community here, and let me tell you young lady, it's a small town. I already have friends saying they are taking their business elsewhere. The talk of the town is how you treated Sharon and your older workers, and if you think this will just blow over in a few weeks, you're nuts.

Don't bother trying to bribe me into staying. Unlike Century, we have more class than that.

You should also know that after Sharon was sacked, after I had just gotten off the phone with my close friend, your subordinate, Aaron Sassower, called me to say he'd give me a five percent discount on some iPads or some other such nonsense. If this was your idea of a sales pitch, you and your team have a lot to learn.

Lots of luck without Sharon. You're going to need it.

X

Jim REARDON

From: KHOURI, Danielle
Sent: October 1, YR-4
To: All
Subject: Re: Employee of the Decade – Sharon Watson

What a tremendous achievement. Congratulations, Sharon! Looking forward to seeing you all at the luncheon!

DK

From: REARDON, Jim
Sent: October 1, YR-4
To: All
Subject: Re: Employee of the Decade – Sharon Watson

Valued employees,

Since founding Century Technologies more than two decades ago, I have seen so many dedicated employees committed to growing this company. This has been a company committed to talent, outperforming our competition, and never settling for second. No one has embodied our commitment to excellence more than Sharon Watson. It is with great pleasure that I announce Sharon has been selected as the Century Technologies Employee of the Decade.

The Board of Directors and I are pleased to invite all of you to a celebratory luncheon in the Nita City Office on October 16 to congratulate Sharon on her years of service and decade of excellence. Lunch and cake will be served, and we will hear from some of Sharon's friends, family, and colleagues.

RSVP to Jane Atkins by October 9 if you are able to attend. Whether you can attend or not, please take a moment to congratulate Sharon on her tremendous achievement.

Best,

Jim Reardon
Founder, Board of Directors

Lou ALDERO

From: STANCIL, Jim
Sent: September 9, YR-4
To: ALDERO, Lou
Subject: RE: Mediation Results

Lou,

I am just doing my job and trying to be fair. I know it's always frustrating when you've got new people with new ideas who don't seem to respect the veterans. Keep in mind—I'm an old dog just like you guys, so I'm in the Sharon boat. I will do my best to make sure these disrespectful comments stop.

Let me know if you have any more problems.

Thanks,

Jim Stancil
Director, Human Resources

From: ALDERO, Lou
Sent: September 9, YR-4
To: STANCIL, Jim
Subject: Mediation Results

Jim,

Just wanted to thank you for your help in mediation yesterday. I know that as an old vet, you've got our backs on these mediations. It's just so tough having these people treating us like this. How are we supposed to feel comfortable in our jobs when old vets like me are getting laid off two at a time and have to come to work to deal with this?

I'm just venting I guess, but I appreciate your help. Let me know if you need any follow-up. This whole thing was probably a misunderstanding, but I want to go on record that this is not OK.

Lou

Exhibit 2

 Amalgamated Pharmaceuticals

A FAMILY CORPORATION
SINCE YR-100

June 21, YR-2

Ms. Danielle Khouri
Century Technologies, Inc.
32 W. Dearborn Avenue
Nita City, Nita

Dear Ms. Khouri:

It is with profound sadness and great dismay that I write you this letter, informing you that Amalgamated Pharmaceuticals will no longer be doing business with Century Technologies. Given our long and prosperous business relationship, I feel it only right I explain my difficult decision more fully.

Recently, Century fired a capable, dedicated, and truly wonderful sales director in Sharon Watson. For us at AmPharm, Sharon was a member of the family. She made us feel valuable every time she picked up the phone. She made personal contacts throughout our office over the last twenty years, and I consider her a close personal friend. Aside from that, she has been a tremendous saleswoman. She had put us first, consistently and reliably, since the beginning.

When I reached out to Century to understand why our most trusted sales person was unceremoniously sacked, I had a conversation with a young man who clearly had no idea how to do business. Aaron Sassower, your new (and from the sound of things, very new) sales director, treated me with none of the respect I have come to expect. He certainly lacked any semblance of the personal touch Sharon always brought to the job. To be blunt, the thought of dealing with Mr. Sassower in the future made it nearly impossible for me and my Board to continue doing business with Century.

I wish you and your fresh, young sales staff all the best in your future endeavors. As a businessman throughout my entire life, I suggest that as you throw Sharon out the door, you take notes on the way she treated people and do your best to emulate her.

Kind regards,

Xavier McDermott

Exhibit 3

MEDIATION REPORT

Date: September 8, YR-4

Parties: Lou Aldero, Ben Dooley

Issue: Inappropriate comments during a meeting

SUMMARY

During a meeting last Wednesday, September 1, YR-4, Ben Dooley and Dakota McKenzie were hosting a New Media Training Session in the Ninth Floor conference center. Lou Aldero and senior staff members of the Southern Division were in town for a conference and attended the training session. I took the following statements related to an incident at that session.

ALDERO: I arrived late to the meeting because I had been at a convention with my staff. Ben made a rude comment as I walked into the room, something to the effect of, "Glad you could join us, Lou." He and others laughed. I don't know why the heck I was singled out. I grabbed a seat, opened my laptop, and began typing in my password. I have an arthritis condition, so typing can be hard, and I use one finger. Ben and Dakota made eye contact and were clearly suppressing a laugh. When Ben continued his presentation, he started typing real slowly with one finger as he was demonstrating ways to update our LinkedIn profiles. The whole room got a huge laugh, and I was totally humiliated. When I asked Ben about it after, he apologized but said I should take it easy.

DOOLEY: While in the middle of a presentation, Lou and his team barged into the conference room and loudly took their seats. It was incredibly disruptive and rude. Lou was still talking while he typed in his password, and so I stopped and stared at him while he did it, not to laugh at him but, you know, to tell him that he should stop in a nonverbal way. When he didn't get that, I started mimicking his typing to get his attention and get him to stop talking. Honestly, I am sorry I hurt his feelings, but he is a grown man who's been at this company since the Truman Administration. I shouldn't have to be a school teacher telling him to behave.

ALDERO: Ben never said anything about being noisy when I came into the room. I didn't realize it was a problem, but I still think he owes me an apology.

CONCLUSION

After hearing both sides of the arguments, I concluded this was not a matter that needed to be referred to superiors. Instead, I had both parties shake hands, and at the end of the meeting both seemed in good spirits.

By signing below, I acknowledge that I have read and reviewed the foregoing statements. I verify that the statements, as recorded, truly and accurately reflect the description of the events at issue, as I relayed them to my human resources mediator. I further attest to and affirm the truth and veracity of these statements as recorded.

B. Dooley
_____
Ben Dooley

Louis M. Aldero
_____
Louis Aldero

MEDIATION REPORT

Date: January 20, YR-3

Parties: Marge Plimpton, Hunter Marten

Issue: Inappropriate comments during a meeting

SUMMARY

After the holidays, January 10, YR-3, Marge Plimpton returned from surgery on her hip. At her desk, there was a hand-drawn sign mimicking a road crossing sign that had an elderly figure crossing a road using a walker. The sign read "Marge Crossing." Marge threw the sign away. Later that week, Marge noticed Hunter Marten imitating her pronounced limp with others in the break room. I took the following statements related to an incident at that session.

PLIMPTON: During the holidays, I had a very painful, but very routine surgery on my hip. I recovered according to schedule, but still had a real limp when I came back. When I had mentioned I'd be getting the surgery, some people joked that I was becoming the old lady in the office, you know, since it was hip surgery. I didn't think much of it. Well, sure enough, on my first day back there's this dumb sign drawn on my desk—it looked like a sign you see on the highway, you know, the yellow ones—that said "Marge Crossing" and "Caution" or something stupid like that. I was so mad I threw it away, but wish I had it. I did my best not to cry and I didn't, but it was incredibly hurtful. I think it was next week, I turned a corner and saw into the break room, and there was Hunter, mocking my limp. He was walking exactly like I had been walking. He and Aaron Sassower and a few others, I can't remember who, were in there. That was so rude and hurtful, but when I told him how it made me feel, he told me I needed to lighten up. He called me "Grandma." It was beyond anything I'd experienced, so I came to Jim and that's it.

MARTEN: I don't know what to say about the sign, because I wasn't the one who drew it. So right off the bat, I feel like it's unfair for me to be in here. I know Marge is bringing that up, but it was probably Aaron or someone much better at drawing than I am. As for the impression, I think this is ridiculous. I was kidding around and wasn't picking on Marge to her face or anything. Even if I had been, I think she is overreacting. I am sorry that she is being so unreasonable, but I still think this is ridiculous. I never come to you, Jim, when they call me "little fella" or "young pup" or whatever it was. Marge was very aggressive and rude when she confronted me, and so I told her to relax and lighten up, which she absolutely should. Again, I'm sorry she blew this out of proportion, but it was just a joke.

PLIMPTON: Well, Jim, now you can see what I'm dealing with. I stand by what I said earlier, this was really rude and inappropriate. And honestly, maybe we'd stop calling Hunter and others "young pups" if they acted like professionals and not frat boys. That's all I can say.

CONCLUSION

After hearing both sides of the arguments, I concluded this was inappropriate. I will refer this to Ben's direct supervisor, Adam Richards, to punish Ben appropriately. I am strongly considering a suspension with pay for this incident. I will consult further with Adam in the days to come.

By signing below, I acknowledge that I have read and reviewed the foregoing statements. I verify that the statements, as recorded, truly and accurately reflect the description of the events at issue, as I relayed them to my human resources mediator. I further attest to and affirm the truth and veracity of these statements as recorded.

MLP
_____
Marge Plimpton

HR Marten
_____
Hunter Marten

Exhibit 4

CENTURY TECHNOLOGIES, INC.

Client Testimonial: Hear What We Have to Offer

Hi, my name is Cynthia Bredemann, and I'm a member of the Century family. I've been a small business owner in Nita City for the last five years, but my business only really started to take off when I joined Century.

I've always been passionate about cooking, and for years friends and family said I was great at it. Finally, I took their advice and started a small food truck in Nita City. At the time, I hardly knew what I was doing, but my hot dogs and hamburgers were the talk of the town. Word of mouth and a good reputation led to lines around the block for my truck—and more customers than I could handle. I decided to hire a staff, purchase a second truck, and just like that, Wheelin' & Mealin' was born.

As my business expanded, I wanted to grow my customer base exponentially. Just using word of mouth wasn't doing it. When I spoke with Century Technologies, they had innovative strategies, software, and hardware to make my dreams a reality. Before I knew it, we had five trucks and had opened a storefront. Through social media and high-powered servers provided by Century, we were able to create a wide network of customers and corporate clients for catering, and our web presence grew by leaps and bounds.

Name:	Cynthia Bredemann
Business:	Wheelin' & Mealin', LLC
Idea:	Providing food on the go through food trucks, pushcarts, storefronts, and deliveries using social media presence and web

Now, we're one of the largest privately owned companies in Nita City, with twenty-four trucks, three storefronts, and a service online that matches hungry people with the cuisine they're looking for that night. None of that would have been possible without Century. I am so lucky to be part of the Century family.

Exhibit 5

May 25, YR-2

Dear Sharon,

I couldn't believe the news. You built this company and this is how they thank you? It's just outrageous. This _must_ be because you're the only adult in the whole office, not to mention the only _real_ sales person. The others treat customers like idiots.

Let me know how I can help. They're not going to get away with this. As your friend for 20 years, I will do whatever you need.

Best, X

Exhibit 6

June YR-2

Sun	Mon	Tue	Wed	Thu	Fri	Sat
					1 *Drinks w/ Sharon*	2
3	4 *Golf w/ Ray*	5	6	7 *Denver Trip* ←	8	9 →
10	11 *Lunch w/ Sharon*	12	13	14	15	16 *Dinner w/ me/Clare + Sharon/ Bill*
17	18 *Interviews* ← →	19	20 *Board meet*	21	22	23
24	25	26	27	28	29 *Clare birthday*	30

Exhibit 7

It's been a great ride, Shar! Have a great day!

Go crazy! Jim

STAY UP PHAT 8:00.

HBD Lisa

HBD :) Dawn

Stay feisty, Happy B'day Mike

Live a fine wine, better yet! Age! Don't listen to Aaron :) Mary

Stay festy, SHARONA. Best, AARON

The world can use a couple more feisty old ladies.

Happy Birthday

Thanks for being a great leader! HBD, Danielle

Exhibit 8

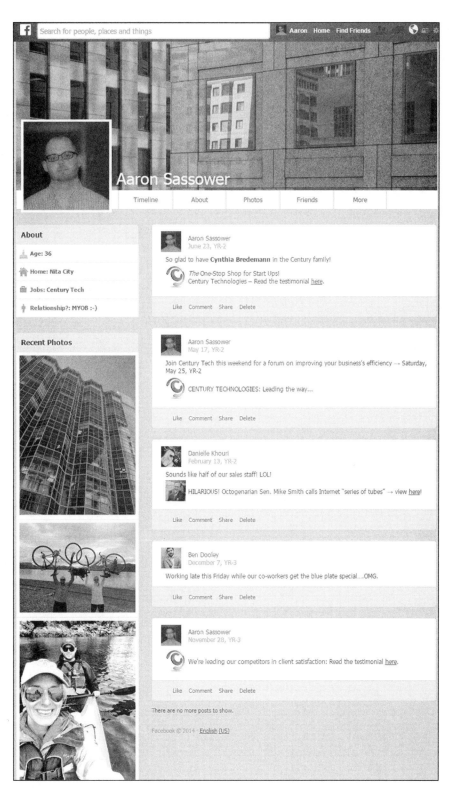

[*See* http://bit.ly/1I7QmTC.]

Exhibit 9

[*See* http://bit.ly/1yGxpiu.]

Exhibit 10

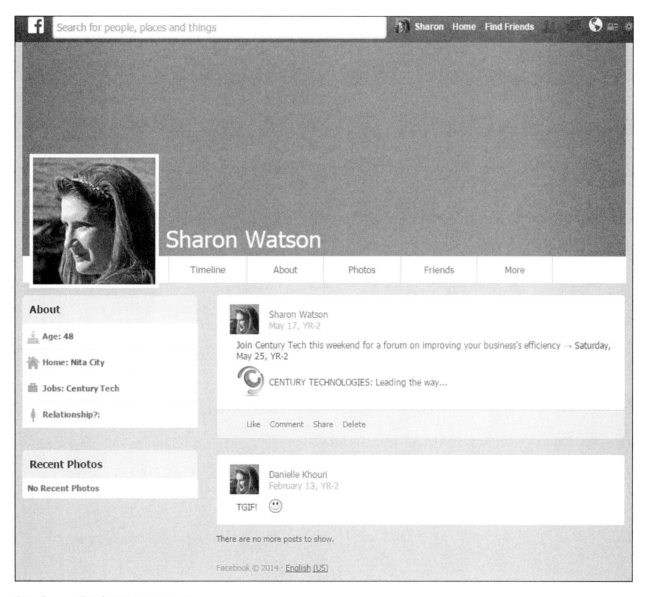

[*See* http://bit.ly/1Hn1CIm.]

Exhibit 11

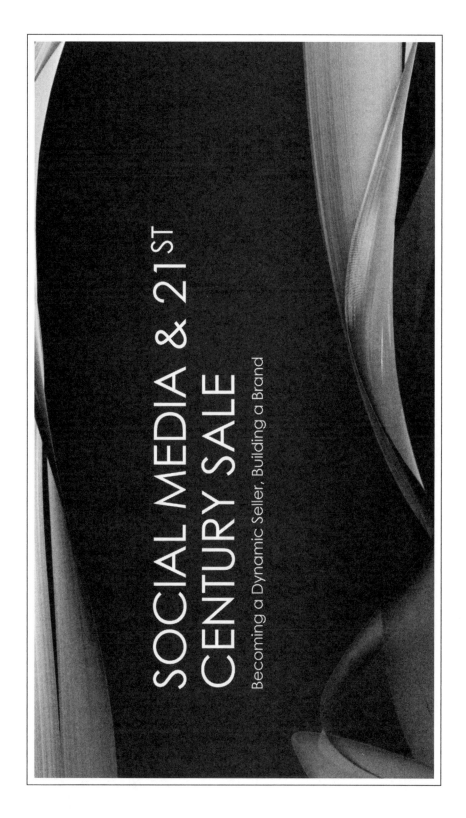

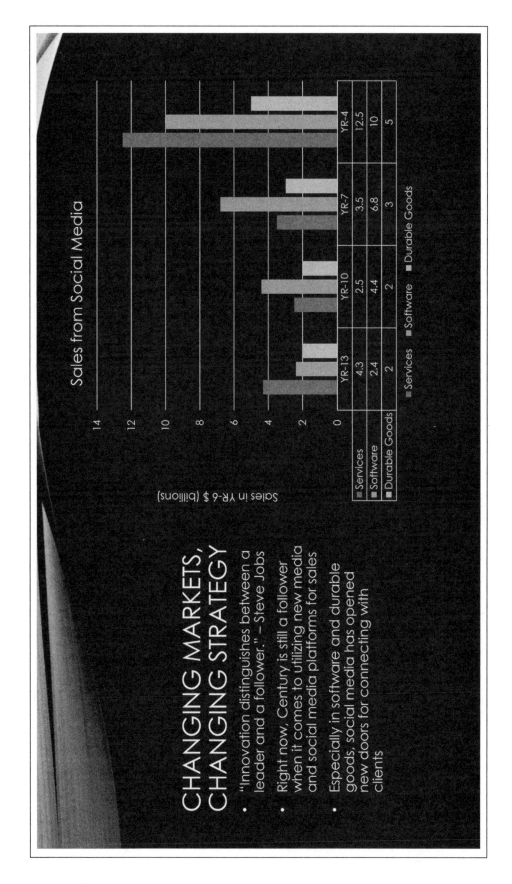

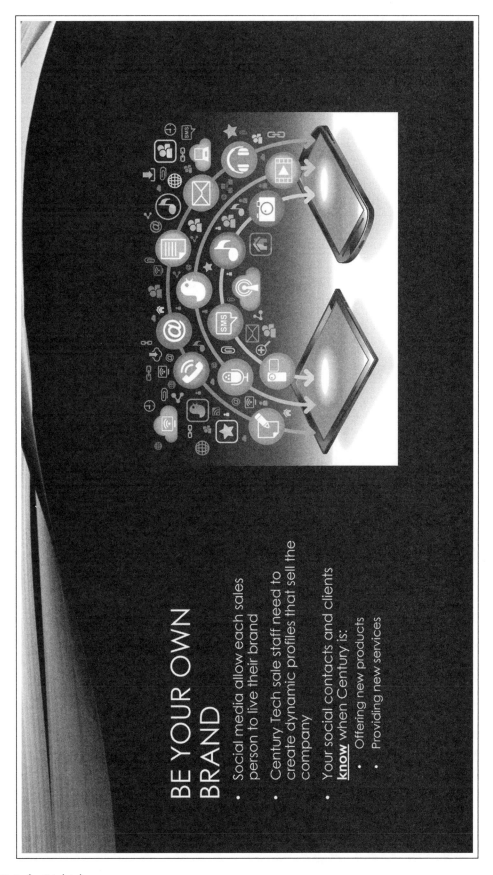

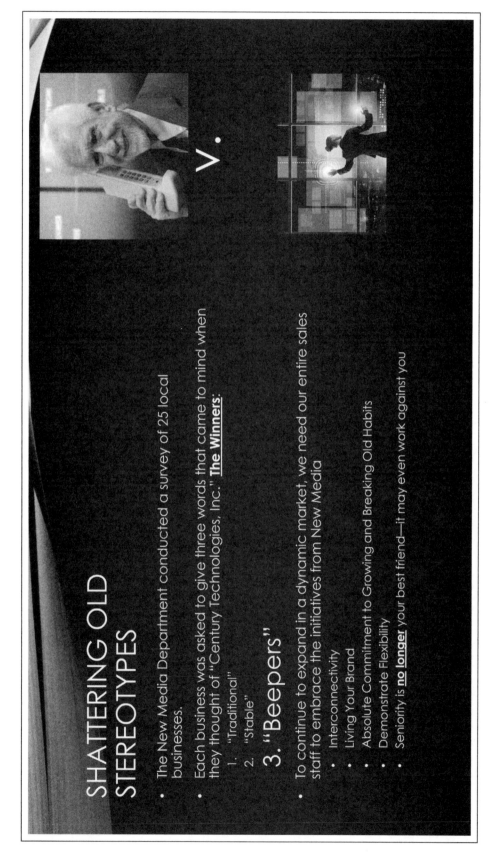

Exhibit 12

Employee:	Watson, Sharon	Employee IDN: 875-41-0952
Position:	Sales Director-NC	Salary: $75,000 Base
		Commission: 2% Gross Sales Above Target
		Bonus: Annual, Reward if Applicable

W-2 – INTERNAL FEDERAL TAX RECORDS, HUMAN RESOURCES

YR-2

Wages:	$31,250.00	Commission:	8,198.65
SS Wages:	39,448.65	SS Withheld:	2,445.82
Medicare Wages:	39,448.65	Medicare Withheld:	572.01
FIC Wages:	39,448.65	FIC Withheld	4,286.05
Bonus:	N/A		

YR-3

Wages:	75,000	Commission:	35,780.01
SS Wages:	110,780.01	SS Withheld:	6,868.36
Medicare Wages:	110,780.01	Medicare Withheld:	1,606.31
FIC Wages:	110,780.01	FIC Withheld	22,099.65
Bonus:	Holiday		

YR-4

Wages:	75,000	Commission:	17,810.84
SS Wages:	92,810.84	SS Withheld:	5,754.27
Medicare Wages:	92,810.84	Medicare Withheld:	1,345.76
FIC Wages:	92,810.84	FIC Withheld	17,156.46
Bonus:	Holiday		

Exhibit 13

CENTURY TECHNOLOGIES, INC.

Annual Sales Report

Fiscal Year YR-2

Region	Oct.	Nov.	Dec.	Jan.	Feb.	March	April	May	June	July	August	Sept.
Northeast	234,632	201,733	154,350	245,610	212,670	89,450	169,221	244,958	148,675	239,163	208,528	220,242
New York	106,216	103,280	191,422	263,926	232,807	173,980	120,501	269,163	115,976	292,721	152,574	121,944
Mid-Atlantic	296,677	174,779	220,902	273,638	154,943	114,296	156,872	200,193	257,303	168,359	135,736	265,944
N. Midwest	278,482	114,818	110,666	139,345	55,512	99,821	191,861	183,993	66,752	124,650	173,838	216,077
Midwest	193,443	248,166	266,682	122,903	294,775	198,138	272,528	236,209	140,924	134,521	103,897	177,448
Nita	85,080	98,100	110,725	208,341	104,216	357,380	206,216	86,766	46,204	186,125	178,900	226,475
Deep South	214,515	86,910	131,185	49,424	120,413	156,433	258,171	98,085	59,707	194,456	78,094	125,143
Mt. West	298,167	157,456	113,982	122,000	141,520	200,153	169,867	77,320	234,530	129,874	207,700	143,112
N. Plains	61,973	95,253	111,261	96,604	106,036	112,929	289,132	130,800	173,996	116,054	130,478	162,557
Pacific	263,408	152,262	101,749	107,726	124,831	149,088	172,029	125,135	209,684	242,886	143,916	218,700

Region	Total Sales
Northeast	2,369,232
New York	2,144,510
Mid-Atlantic	2,419,642
N. Midwest	1,755,815
Midwest	2,389,634
Nita	1,894,528
Deep South	1,572,536
Mt. West	1,995,681
N. Plains	1,587,073
Pacific	2,011,414

CENTURY TECHNOLOGIES, INC.

Annual Sales Report

Fiscal Year YR-3

Region	Oct.	Nov.	Dec.	Jan.	Feb.	March	April	May	June	July	August	Sept.
Northeast	194,801	110,000	89,560	98,430	88,490	120,450	107,400	189,300	181,405	94,350	81,900	138,150
New York	216,754	202,634	185,100	177,050	159,280	89,230	120,400	123,450	118,920	112,780	75,300	144,900
Mid-Atlantic	112,800	114,870	110,900	112,500	127,300	180,325	144,018	210,633	236,043	190,481	253,099	121,850
N. Midwest	192,953	171,534	115,110	198,324	150,972	276,797	182,894	140,709	158,655	85,309	179,688	84,929
Midwest	197,336	211,399	206,546	199,324	211,300	263,691	88,211	118,001	184,629	207,931	117,125	121,375
Nita	309,852	317,009	318,747	289,152	282,796	381,606	294,687	342,560	327,890	317,837	286,426	308,449
Deep South	155,839	255,156	273,653	193,108	180,927	174,182	236,954	193,305	172,311	130,992	166,374	213,955
Mt. West	194,139	175,356	293,207	160,383	265,100	189,577	99,029	215,197	296,550	77,912	158,634	251,023
N. Plains	140,420	207,520	130,041	153,917	279,731	178,832	201,996	241,514	193,076	93,543	109,636	175,316
Pacific	98,326	178,257	292,331	174,004	261,950	288,099	226,864	116,187	177,937	110,001	120,615	133,200

Region	Total Sales
Northeast	1,494,236
New York	1,725,798
Mid-Atlantic	1,914,819
N. Midwest	1,937,874
Midwest	2,126,868
Nita	3,777,011
Deep South	2,346,756
Mt. West	2,376,107
N. Plains	2,105,542
Pacific	2,177,771

CENTURY TECHNOLOGIES, INC.

Annual Sales Report

Fiscal Year YR-4

Region	Oct.	Nov.	Dec.	Jan.	Feb.	March	April	May	June	July	August	Sept.
Northeast	205,752	110,000	89,560	98,430	88,490	120,450	107,400	74,500	92,200	94,350	81,900	138,150
New York	264,499	255,526	185,100	177,050	159,280	89,230	120,400	123,450	118,920	112,780	75,300	144,900
Mid-Atlantic	112,800	114,870	110,900	112,500	127,300	96,187	215,531	244,427	233,867	148,494	181,897	73,117
N. Midwest	187,754	118,041	135,326	139,929	181,521	178,200	75,169	91,503	175,439	225,919	241,014	114,976
Midwest	143,544	102,071	261,661	118,992	211,300	166,522	177,486	106,242	75,382	79,663	219,195	127,626
Nita	175,993	167,470	170,287	175,993	230,672	306,357	175,080	196,521	189,450	247,800	98,791	175,993
Deep South	71,580	213,110	222,450	195,880	126,867	203,869	257,227	259,091	292,252	276,928	221,392	215,472
Mt. West	192,309	181,154	85,376	209,940	115,482	74,227	70,240	147,358	254,656	181,341	263,362	83,606
N. Plains	199,191	189,024	81,944	294,414	77,172	214,286	82,981	224,004	299,924	112,882	276,898	207,578
Pacific	299,505	111,118	160,639	242,263	244,110	188,159	77,564	138,060	208,664	193,200	182,765	152,031

Region	Total Sales
Northeast	1,301,182
New York	1,826,435
Mid-Atlantic	1,771,890
N. Midwest	1,864,791
Midwest	1,789,684
Nita	2,310,407
Deep South	2,556,118
Mt. West	1,859,051
N. Plains	2,260,298
Pacific	2,198,078

Exhibit 14

CENTURY TECHNOLOGIES, INC.

EMPLOYMENT MANUAL

V. POLICY AGAINST WORK PLACE HARASSMENT

Century Technologies prides itself on inclusiveness, respect, and harmony in the workplace. To that end, Century maintains a strong policy against harassment of any kind in the office. Additionally, our policies against harassment extend beyond the walls of the building. Employees and supervisors alike must remain respectful of other Century employees *at all times*.

Century's firm commitment begins with the acknowledgment that harassment of any kind may be unlawful in the State of Nita. To reinforce this commitment, Century has developed a policy against harassment and a reporting procedure for employees who have been subjected to or witnessed harassment. Century firmly believes that all employees have a duty to fight harassment: if you see something, say something! This policy applies to all work-related settings and activities, whether inside or outside the workplace, and includes business trips and business-related social events.

Our policy extends to every level of the Century family: from directors and officers, to customers and vendors.

Prohibition of Sexual Harassment

Century's policy against sexual harassment prohibits sexual advances or requests for sexual favors or other physical or verbal conduct of a sexual nature, when: (1) submission to such conduct is made an express or implicit condition of employment; (2) submission to or rejection of such conduct is used as a basis for employment decisions affecting the individual who submits to or rejects such conduct; or (3) such conduct has the purpose or effect of unreasonably interfering with an employee's work performance or creating an intimidating, hostile, humiliating, or offensive working environment.

While such behavior, depending on the circumstances, may not be severe or pervasive enough to create a sexually hostile work environment, it can nonetheless make coworkers uncomfortable. Accordingly, such behavior is inappropriate and may result in disciplinary action regardless of whether it is unlawful. It is also unlawful and expressly against Century policy to retaliate against an employee for filing a complaint of sexual harassment or for cooperating with an investigation of a complaint of sexual harassment.

Prohibition of Other Types of Discriminatory Harassment

Century's policy strictly forbids verbal or physical conduct that shows hostility toward an individual because of his or her race, color, gender, religion, sexual orientation, age, national origin, disability, or other protected category of the Nita Civil Rights Act that: (1) has the purpose or effect of creating an intimidating, humiliating, or offensive office environment; (2) has the purpose or effect of interfering with an individual's work performance; or (3) otherwise negatively impacts an individual's employment opportunities.

Century reserves the right to determine whether or not conduct constitutes discriminatory harassment on a case by case basis.

Reporting of Harassment

If you believe that you have experienced or witnessed sexual harassment or other discriminatory harassment by any employee of Century, you shall report the incident immediately to your supervisor or to the Director of Human Resources (HR) and file a written complaint on Century Tech Form C-1211. If the Director of HR is the perpetrator of the harassment, report the incident to any other HR personnel, and that employee will direct the matter to the appropriate executive. Possible harassment by others with whom Century has a business relationship, including customers and vendors, should also be reported as soon as possible so that appropriate action can be taken.

Century will promptly and thoroughly investigate all reports of harassment as discreetly and confidentially as practicable. The investigation *must* include: (1) a private interview with the person making a report of harassment and (2) a private interview with the person accused of harassment. It would also generally be necessary to discuss the incident with others who may have information relevant to the investigation. Century's goal is to conduct a thorough investigation, to determine whether discrimination occurred, and to determine what action to take if it is determined that improper behavior occurred.

If Century determines that a violation of this policy has occurred, it will take appropriate disciplinary action against the offending party, which can include counseling, warnings, suspensions, and termination. Additionally, when appropriate, the Director of HR will require both or all parties involved to resolve disputes through mediation. Employees who report violations of this policy and employees who cooperate with investigations into alleged violations of this policy *will not be subject to retaliation*. Upon completion of any investigation, Century must inform the employee who made the complaint of the results of the investigation. Compliance with this policy is a condition of each employee's employment. Employees are encouraged to raise any questions or concerns about this policy or about possible discriminatory harassment with the Director of HR. In the case where the allegation of harassment is against the Director of HR, please notify a subordinate HR employee and that employee will handle the matter accordingly.

CENTURY TECHNOLOGIES, INC.

Claimant:_____   Offender:_____

Conduct Alleged:_____   Witnesses (?):_____

Date of Incident:_____   Location of Incident: _____

FOR HR USE ONLY: Violation Code: _____   Superior:_____

　　　　　Interview Date: _____   Resolution:_____

STATEMENT:

_____
_____
_____
_____
_____
_____
_____
_____
_____
_____
_____
_____
_____
_____
_____

_____   _____
Date   Claimant

DEPOSITIONS

Danielle Khouri

Page 1

```
 1              IN THE UNITED STATES DISTRICT COURT
 2         FOR THE DISTRICT OF NITA CITY, NITA
 3                    CIVIL DIVISION
 4                    ---oOo---
 5
 6
 7    SHARON WATSON 6232 N. Ionia
 8    Avenue, Nita City, Nita
 9                                 )
10         Plaintiff,     ) Case No. CAL:
11       vs.              ) 2011-CIV-10886
11    CENTURY TECHNOLOGIES, INC., 32 )
12    W. Dearborn Street, Nita City, )
13    Nita,                          )
14              Defendant.           )
15
16
17
18                    ---oOo---
19         MONDAY, OCTOBER 7, YR-1
20    DEPOSITION OF DANIELLE ERIN KHOURI
21                    ---oOo---
22
23
24
25    REPORTER: BALINDA DUNLAP, CSR 10710, RPR, CRR, RMR
```

Page 2

```
 1         NITA CITY, NITA OCTOBER 7, YR-1
 2                    ---oOo---
 3         BE IT REMEMBERED that on Monday, the 7th
 4    day of October YR-1, commencing at the hour of
 5    11:30 a.m. thereof, at Barkley Court Reporters, 201
 6    California Street, Suite 375, Nita City, Nita,
 7    before me, Balinda Dunlap, a Certified
 8    Shorthand Reporter in and for Nita City
 9    State of Nita, personally
10    appeared:
11              DANIELLE ERIN KHOURI
12         a Witness herein; called as a witness; who,
13    after having been duly sworn by the Certified
14    Shorthand Reporter to tell the truth, the whole
15    truth, and nothing but the truth, testified as
16    follows:
17                    ---oOo---
18    Q.  Please state your full name for the
19    record.
20    A.  Danielle Erin Khouri.
21    Q.  What is your current address?
22    A.  724 E. Oak Street, Nita City,
23    Nita.
24    Q.  Do you live alone?
25    A.  Yes, I do.
```

Page 3

```
 1    Q.  Are you married?
 2    A.  No. I just said I live alone.
 3    Q.  Very good. Have you ever been married?
 4    A.  Yes. I was married for six years, but I
 5    am recently divorced.
 6    Q.  What is your current occupation?
 7    A.  I am the Chief Executive Officer of
 8    Century Technologies.
 9    Q.  What are your day to day duties as Chief
10    Officer?
11    A.  I run the show. I don't know how to --
12    Q.  Of course, Ms. Khouri, but can you just
13    describe some of your responsibilities?
14    A.  Yes. I am in charge of strategy decisions
15    for the company. Products we hope to sell. I
16    occasionally handle major client development and
17    retention. A large part of my responsibility is
18    being the face and voice of the company.
19    Q.  For how long have you been the CEO?
20    A.  I am about to have my third anniversary as
21    head of Century.
22    Q.  Congratulations. What was your profession
23    before joining Century?
24    A.  You mean before I was CEO or before I came
25    to Century?
```

Page 4

```
 1    Q.  Let's start with before you came to
 2    Century. Where were you before joining Century?
 3    A.  I started out after college as an
 4    executive at Global Equity Strategies in
 5    California.
 6    Q.  What did you do for them?
 7    A.  Just your entry-level analyst position. I
 8    studied markets, tried to find solid investment
 9    opportunities, brought them to the higher-ups to
10    sort out.
11    Q.  Did you need a degree for that position?
12    A.  I went to Stanford Business School, so
13    yeah, I needed a degree.
14    Q.  Did you get the position at Global Equity
15    right out of school?
16    A.  Yes. They have a strong recruiting
17    presence on campus.
18    Q.  How did you end up joining Century?
19    A.  Well, part of my position involved
20    studying the technology sector to find
21    underperforming companies to invest in. Century
22    was on our radar screen.
23    Q.  Can you say when this was?
24    A.  Sure. I graduated college in YR-14. I was
25    at Global for about two or three years when we got
```

SHARON WATSON vs.
CENTURY TECHNOLOGIES, INC.

DANIELLE ERIN KHOURI
October 7, YR-1

Page 5

1   interested in Century.
2   Q. What sparked your interest in Century?
3   A. Well, they had a solid client base, strong
4   revenues, but it just seemed like they weren't
5   getting the best out of their staff.
6   Q. What made you think that?
7   A. I crunched the numbers. I spoke with some
8   of my supervisors who had been doing this much
9   longer than I had been. Something just wasn't
10   right.
11   Q. What did you do?
12   A. I met with several executives over at
13   Century. By this time, I had already been promoted
14   to junior vice president at Global, so I had some
15   say in how we invested.
16   Q. What did your conversations entail?
17   A. Well, I met with Century people to get a
18   better feel for their products, their methods,
19   their staff. I just saw a lot of redundancy and a
20   total unwillingness to change.
21   Q. After just a few meetings?
22   A. It was that obvious, yes.
23   Q. What did you do with this information?
24   A. I took it to my superiors, but everyone's
25   heads were still spinning from the dot-com burst.

Page 6

1   No one wanted anything to do with a tech sales and
2   consulting firm.
3   Q. How did you ultimately end up at Century?
4   A. I must have impressed the Board when I met
5   with them, because they offered me a position in
6   YR-9.
7   Q. What was the position?
8   A. Well, they created it just for me. I was
9   going to be the Vice President of New Media. It
10   was just a title, because what they really wanted
11   was for me to rework the company.
12   Q. How did you go about doing that?
13   A. I started seeing where there were
14   inefficiencies. At every company, there's
15   somewhere you can start trimming the fat.
16   Q. When did you first meet Sharon Watson?
17   A. I met Sharon at one of my initial meetings
18   with all the Regional Sales Directors and Assistant
19   Regional Sales Directors.
20   Q. When was that?
21   A. So I came on board in August YR-9, and our
22   first Century Convention was in August YR-9.
23   That's when I met Sharon.
24   Q. Do you remember anything about your
25   encounter?

Page 7

1   A. No, not really. We didn't interact much
2   personally. At that time, I just wanted to meet
3   the sales personnel to give them a sense of where
4   the company was going.
5   Q. What did you tell them?
6   A. I said that the future was bright for the
7   company, and for anyone willing to grow with it. I
8   let them know we would be changing and that I
9   looked forward to making contributions.
10   Q. How did they take that?
11   A. As well as could be expected. Some
12   27-year-old waltzes into their lives and tells them
13   they're changing things up. How would anyone take
14   it?
15   Q. What part did you play in these changes?
16   A. The Board brought me in to make changes.
17   So when I suggested new strategies or development
18   areas, they sent the orders to executives and then to
19   Regional Directors.
20   Q. You didn't give any orders personally?
21   A. Oh, God, no. Like I said, these were old
22   salts who had been doing business since the beeper
23   days. They weren't going to take advice from me.
24   I was mainly behind the scenes.
25   Q. What were some initiatives you started?

Page 8

1   A. There was a lot of dead weight. People
2   who had been there years and were getting stubborn
3   and set in their ways just held the company back.
4   We eliminated a few positions early on.
5   Q. How did that go?
6   A. Obviously, it was hard. But sometimes,
7   eliminating dead weight can get others motivated to
8   change and adapted.
9   Q. Did that happen?
10   A. Yes and no. I mean, Rome wasn't built in
11   a day.
12   Q. What other changes took place?
13   A. I wanted all the sales staff to get more
14   involved in social media. This is right when
15   Facebook and other social media platforms were
16   blowing up. I had Aaron Sassower and some others
17   who joined us later start training regularly.
18   Q. Do you have a Facebook profile?
19   A. I do. But as the CEO, I don't do as much
20   Facebooking as I encourage my sales directors to
21   do.
22   Q. How much Facebooking do you want them to
23   do?
24   A. I don't set some kind of target. I
25   just tell them that they should be the face of

Page 9

1   Century at all times.
2   Q.   What did you do to teach the older sales
3   staff to get involved?
4   A.   We knew it wouldn't be easy. It's tough
5   to teach an old dog new tricks, but we certainly
6   tried. We had seminars, PowerPoints, regular
7   instructional meetings from our newer, younger
8   go-getters on getting into the social media game.
9   Q.   How did that go?
10 A.   About as I expected. Some rolled their
11 eyes, others adapted and thrived. The eye-rollers
12 found themselves looking for new jobs.
13 Q.   Simply because they wouldn't get into
14 social media?
15 A.   Because they were stuck in their ways and
16 refused to grow. We weren't selling fax machines
17 door to door here. I was trying to build a
18 company.
19 Q.   How did Sharon Watson take your
20 suggestions?
21 A.   She was hard to read. I had conversations
22 with her supervisor, and he always said she
23 wasn't on board. It upset me.
24 Q.   Why?
25 A.   Because she was a talented salesperson,

Page 10

1   but without my suggestions, she wasn't reaching her
2   potential. She had so much knowledge, but lacked
3   the drive.
4   Q.   Did she get on Facebook?
5   A.   She did.
6   Q.   And her sales were strong?
7   A.   They were fine. They weren't spectacular
8   considering her market was Nita and her
9   certificate was huge.
10 Q.   Was she not named Employee of the Decade
11 in YR-4?
12 A.   Sure she was, but I mean, that was because
13 of her longevity. She wasn't reinventing the
14 wheel. She sold a lot of PCs.
15 Q.   What other interactions did you have with
16 Sharon Watson before being named CEO?
17 A.   I'd see her around the office now and
18 then. We were always friendly with each other. I
19 knew people respected her, even though she didn't
20 respect me.
21 Q.   Why didn't she respect you?
22 A.   She'd been making comments about the
23 "young pups" in the office with all our new ideas.
24 She was just old school and not willing to change.
25 Q.   When were you named CEO?

Page 11

1   A.   The Board installed me as CEO just after
2   New Year's in YR-3.
3   Q.   What were your priorities?
4   A.   I wanted to make sure that our sales
5   stayed steady while we expanded our client base
6   beyond brick and mortar stores. That meant
7   aggressive web presence.
8   Q.   How did you implement that strategy?
9   A.   Well, as VP of New Media, I tiptoed and
10 tried to get things done behind the scenes. As
11 CEO, I was off the leash. It was a brave new
12 world.
13 Q.   What were some of your first actions?
14 A.   Further cuts to the old vets who didn't
15 like my ideas.
16 Q.   Why was that your first move?
17 A.   I had to send a message that we were
18 moving in a new direction. I wanted all my
19 employees, young and old, to know that they could
20 get on board or get out.
21 Q.   How many employees did you let go?
22 A.   I can't remember. I wasn't a blood bath
23 or anything. It was just to send a message.
24 Q.   Why not Sharon Watson?
25 A.   Her numbers were good, and I thought she'd

Page 12

1   eventually come around.
2   Q.   Did you hear about any of the complaints
3   regarding younger employees harassing older
4   employees?
5   A.   Just office politics and bad jokes gone
6   wrong.
7   Q.   But you heard about them?
8   A.   Yes. I heard a lot from younger employees
9   of being disrespected as well. It was a
10 generational struggle here.
11 Q.   What did your younger employees say?
12 A.   We exchanged emails, just standard stuff.
13 Eye-rolling in meetings was a big complaint. There
14 were a few outbursts, too.
15 Q.   Can you name a specific time?
16 A.   Aaron Sassower gave some presentation with
17 a picture of a dinosaur on it.
18 Q.   Did Sharon ever speak to you regarding a
19 transfer?
20 A.   She did.
21 Q.   What was your response?
22 A.   We needed her, and she wasn't going
23 anywhere.
24 Q.   Did you investigate the possibility of a
25 transfer?

Page 13

1 A. No. I knew we couldn't spare her.
2 Q. But you didn't even investigate?
3 A. I didn't need to. I knew our
4 availability.
5 Q. How did she take it?
6 A. Not well, but I wasn't surprised.
7 Q. Why not?
8 A. She wasn't getting along with the new
9 employees. It was pretty surprising and
10 disappointing.
11 Q. How could you tell?
12 A. She was constantly complaining, and then
13 when we promoted Dakota, she completely lost her
14 mind.
15 Q. Can you elaborate?
16 A. She came into my office when we promoted
17 Dakota Mackenzie to COO and started yelling at me.
18 Q. When did this happen?
19 A. February YR-2.
20 Q. How was that decision made?
21 A. Dakota's an amazing talent, rose up
22 through the ranks quickly. She impressed the right
23 people.
24 Q. Did you consider Sharon?
25 A. No.

Page 14

1 Q. How did she approach you when she learned
2 the news?
3 A. She exploded. She called me a liar. Told
4 me I had no idea how to run the company. I
5 couldn't believe her behavior.
6 Q. What did you say to her?
7 A. I told her she needed to calm down before
8 she said something she regretted.
9 Q. How did she take that?
10 A. Kept yelling, refused to leave my office.
11 It was such a shame to see her break down like
12 that.
13 Q. How did you handle the situation?
14 A. I told her no one was bigger than the
15 company, that I respected her history with the
16 company, but we didn't have room for inflexibility.
17 Q. How did she react?
18 A. Stormed out, and then from that pointed
19 on, everything changed.
20 Q. In what way?
21 A. She was sullen, just kind of difficult
22 until we finally had to let her go last year.
23 Q. Did age play a factor in your decision?
24 A. No. Her attitude did.
25

Page 15

1 DEPOSITION OFFICER'S CERTIFICATE
2 NITA CITY   )
3 STATE OF NITA) ss.
4
5
6 I, Balinda Dunlap, hereby certify:
7 I am a duly qualified Certified Shorthand
8 Reporter in the State of Nita, holder of
9 Certificate Number CSR 10710 issued by the Court
10 Reporters Board of Nita and which is in full force
11 and effect. (Fed. R. Civ. P. 28(a)).
12 I am authorized to administer
13 oaths or affirmations pursuant to Nita Code of
14 Civil Procedure, Section 2093(b) and prior to being
15 examined, the witness was first duly sworn by me.
16 (Fed. R. Civ. P. 28(2), 30(f)(1)).
17 I am not a relative or employee or attorney or
18 counsel of any of the parties, nor am I a relative or
19 employee of such attorney or counsel, nor am I
20 financially interested in this action. (Fed. R. Civ. P.
21 28).
22 I am the deposition officer that
23 stenographically recorded the testimony in the foregoing
24 deposition and the foregoing transcript is a true record
25 / / /

Page 16

1 of the testimony given by the witness. (Fed. R. Civ. P.
2 30(f)(1)).
3 Before completion of the deposition, review of
4 the transcript [ ] was [ ] was not requested. If
5 requested, any changes made by the deponent (and
6 provided to the reporter) during the period allowed, are
7 appended hereto. (Fed. R. Civ. P. 30(e)).
8
9 Dated: October 21, YR-1
10
11 _____
12
13
14
15
16
17
18
19
20
21
22
23
24
25

SHARON WATSON vs.
CENTURY TECHNOLOGIES, INC.

DANIELLE ERIN KHOURI
October 7, YR-1

A

Aaron (2)
8:16;12:16
actions (1)
11:13
adapted (2)
8:8;9:11
address (1)
2:21
advice (1)
7:23
age (1)
14:23
aggressive (1)
11:7
alone (2)
2:24;3:2
along (1)
13:8
always (2)
9:22;10:18
amazing (1)
13:21
analyst (1)
4:7
anniversary (1)
3:20
appeared (1)
2:10
approach (1)
14:1
areas (1)
7:18
around (2)
10:17;12:1
Assistant (1)
6:18
attitude (1)
14:24
August (1)
6:21
availability (1)
13:4

B

back (1)
8:3
bad (1)
12:5
Balinda (1)
2:7
Barkley (1)
2:5
base (2)
5:3;11:5
bath (1)
11:22
beeper (1)
7:22
behavior (1)

14:5
behind (2)
7:24;11:10
better (1)
5:18
beyond (1)
11:6
big (1)
12:13
bigger (1)
14:14
blood (1)
11:22
blowing (1)
8:16
Board (6)
6:4,21;7:16;9:23;
11:1,20
brave (1)
11:11
break (1)
14:11
brick (1)
11:6
bright (1)
7:6
brought (2)
4:9;7:16
build (1)
9:17
built (1)
8:10
Business (2)
4:12;7:22

C

CALIFORNIA (5)
2:1,6,7,9;4:5
called (2)
2:12;14:3
calm (1)
14:7
came (4)
3:24;4:1;6:21;13:16
campus (1)
4:17
can (6)
3:12;4:23;6:15;8:7;
12:15;13:15
Century (15)
3:8,21,23,25;4:2,2,
18,21;5:1,2,13,17;6:3,
22;9:1
CEO (7)
3:19,24;8:19;10:16,
25;11:1,11
certainly (1)
9:5
certificate (1)
10:9
Certified (2)
2:7,13

change (3)
5:20;8:8;10:24
changed (1)
14:19
changes (3)
7:15,16;8:12
changing (2)
7:8,13
charge (1)
3:14
Chief (2)
3:7,9
client (3)
3:16;5:3;11:5
college (2)
4:3,24
Columbia (2)
2:23;10:8
com (1)
5:25
commencing (1)
2:4
comments (1)
10:22
companies (1)
4:21
company (11)
3:15,18;6:11,14;7:4,
7;8:3;9:18;14:4,15,16
complaining (1)
13:12
complaint (1)
12:13
complaints (1)
12:2
completely (1)
13:13
Congratulations (1)
3:22
consider (1)
13:24
considering (1)
10:8
constantly (1)
13:12
consulting (1)
6:2
contributions (1)
7:9
Convention (1)
6:22
conversations (2)
5:16;9:21
COO (1)
13:17
County (1)
2:8
course (1)
3:12
Court (1)
2:5
created (1)
6:8

crunched (1)
5:7
current (2)
2:21;3:6
cuts (1)
11:14

D

Dakota (2)
13:13,17
Dakota's (1)
13:21
DANIELLE (2)
2:11,20
day (4)
2:4;3:9,9;8:11
days (1)
7:23
dead (2)
8:1,7
Decade (1)
10:10
decision (2)
13:20;14:23
decisions (1)
3:14
degree (2)
4:11,13
describe (1)
3:13
development (2)
3:16;7:17
difficult (1)
14:21
dinosaur (1)
12:17
direction (1)
11:18
Directors (4)
6:18,19;7:19;8:20
disappointing (1)
13:10
disrespected (1)
12:9
divorced (1)
3:5
dog (1)
9:5
done (1)
11:10
door (2)
9:17,17
dot (1)
5:25
double (1)
5:25
down (2)
14:7,11
drive (1)
10:3
duly (1)
2:13

Dunlap (1)
2:7
duties (1)
3:9

E

early (1)
8:4
easy (1)
9:4
elaborate (1)
13:15
eliminated (1)
8:4
eliminating (1)
8:7
emails (1)
12:12
employees (7)
11:19,21;12:3,4,8,
11;13:9
encounter (1)
6:25
encourage (1)
8:20
end (2)
4:18;6:3
entail (1)
5:16
entry-level (1)
4:7
Equity (2)
4:4,14
ERIN (2)
2:11,20
even (2)
10:19;13:2
eventually (1)
12:1
everyone's (1)
5:24
exchanged (1)
12:12
Executive (3)
3:7;4:4;10:10
executives (2)
5:12;7:18
expanded (1)
11:5
expected (2)
7:11;9:10
exploded (1)
14:3
eye-rollers (1)
9:11
Eye-rolling (1)
12:13
eyes (1)
9:11

F

Barkley Court Reporters

(1) Aaron - eyes

face (2)
3:18;8:25
factor (1)
14:23
fat (1)
6:15
fax (1)
9:16
February (1)
13:19
feel (1)
5:18
few (3)
5:21;8:4;12:14
finally (1)
14:22
find (2)
4:8,20
fine (1)
10:7
firm (1)
6:2
first (4)
6:16,22;11:13,16
follows (1)
2:16
forward (1)
7:9
found (1)
9:12
FRANCISCO (3)
2:1,6,9
friendly (1)
10:18
full (1)
2:18
Further (1)
11:14
future (1)
7:6

G

game (1)
9:8
gave (1)
12:16
generational (1)
12:10
Global (4)
4:4,14,25;5:14
God (1)
7:21
go-getters (1)
9:8
good (2)
3:3;11:25
graduated (1)
4:24
grow (2)
7:7;9:16

H

handle (2)
3:16;14:13
happen (2)
8:9;13:18
harassing (1)
12:3
hard (2)
8:6;9:21
head (1)
3:21
heads (1)
5:25
hear (1)
12:2
heard (2)
12:7,8
held (1)
8:3
herein (1)
2:12
higher-ups (1)
4:9
history (1)
14:15
hope (1)
3:15
hour (1)
2:4
huge (1)
10:9

I

idea (1)
14:4
ideas (2)
10:23;11:15
implement (1)
11:8
impressed (2)
6:4;13:22
inefficiencies (1)
6:14
inflexibility (1)
14:16
information (1)
5:23
initial (1)
6:17
initiatives (1)
7:25
installed (1)
11:1
instructional (1)
9:7
interact (1)
7:1
interactions (1)
10:15
interest (1)

5:2
interested (1)
5:1
into (4)
7:12;9:8,13;13:16
invest (1)
4:21
invested (1)
5:15
investigate (2)
12:24;13:2
investment (1)
4:8
involved (3)
4:19;8:14;9:3

J

jobs (1)
9:12
joined (1)
8:17
joining (3)
3:23;4:2,18
jokes (1)
12:5
junior (1)
5:14

K

Kept (1)
14:10
KHOURI (3)
2:11,20;3:12
kind (2)
8:24;14:21
knew (4)
9:4;10:19;13:1,3
knowledge (1)
10:2

L

lacked (1)
10:2
large (1)
3:17
last (1)
14:22
later (1)
8:17
learned (1)
14:1
leash (1)
11:11
leave (1)
14:10
liar (1)
14:3
live (2)
2:24;3:2
lives (1)

7:12
long (1)
3:19
longer (1)
5:9
longevity (1)
10:13
looked (1)
7:9
looking (1)
9:12
lost (1)
13:13
lot (4)
5:19;8:1;10:14;12:8

M

machines (1)
9:16
Mackenzie (1)
13:17
mainly (1)
7:24
major (1)
3:16
making (2)
7:9;10:22
many (1)
11:21
market (1)
10:8
markets (1)
4:8
married (3)
3:1,3,4
mean (3)
3:24;8:10;10:12
meant (1)
11:6
Media (6)
6:9;8:14,15;9:8,14;
11:9
meet (2)
6:16;7:2
meetings (4)
5:21;6:17;9:7;12:13
message (2)
11:17,23
met (5)
5:12,17;6:4,17,23
methods (1)
5:18
mind (1)
13:14
Monday (1)
2:3
more (1)
8:13
mortar (1)
11:6
motivated (1)
8:7

move (1)
11:16
moving (1)
11:18
much (5)
5:8;7:1;8:19,22;10:2
must (1)
6:4

N

name (2)
2:18;12:15
named (3)
10:10,16,25
need (2)
4:11;13:3
needed (3)
4:13;12:22;14:7
New (12)
2:22;6:9;7:17;9:5,
12;10:8,23;11:2,9,11,
18;13:8
newer (1)
9:7
news (1)
14:2
November (1)
6:22
numbers (2)
5:7;11:25

O

o0o- (2)
2:2,17
Oak (1)
2:22
obvious (1)
5:22
Obviously (1)
8:6
occasionally (1)
3:16
occupation (1)
3:6
OCTOBER (2)
2:1,4
off (1)
11:11
offered (1)
6:5
office (5)
10:17,23;12:5;13:16;
14:10
Officer (2)
3:7,10
offing (1)
8:24
old (5)
7:21;9:5;10:24;
11:14,19
older (2)

9:2;12:3
one (3)
  6:1,17;14:14
opportunities (1)
  4:9
orders (2)
  7:18,20
others (3)
  8:7,16;9:11
out (6)
  4:3,10,15;5:5;11:20;
  14:18
outbursts (1)
  12:14
over (1)
  5:12

P

part (3)
  3:17;4:19;7:15
PCs (1)
  10:14
people (4)
  5:17;8:1;10:19;
  13:23
personally (3)
  2:9;7:2,20
personnel (1)
  7:3
picture (1)
  12:17
place (1)
  8:12
platforms (1)
  8:15
play (2)
  7:15;14:23
Please (1)
  2:18
pointed (1)
  14:18
politics (1)
  12:5
position (6)
  4:7,11,14,19;6:5,7
positions (1)
  8:4
possibility (1)
  12:24
potential (1)
  10:2
PowerPoints (1)
  9:6
presence (2)
  4:17;11:7
presentation (1)
  12:16
president (2)
  5:14;6:9
pretty (1)
  13:9
priorities (1)

11:3
Products (2)
  3:15;5:18
profession (1)
  3:22
profile (1)
  8:18
promoted (3)
  5:13;13:13,16
pups (1)
  10:23

Q

quickly (1)
  13:22

R

radar (1)
  4:22
ranks (1)
  13:22
reaching (1)
  10:1
react (1)
  14:17
read (1)
  9:21
really (2)
  6:10;7:1
recently (1)
  3:5
record (1)
  2:19
recruiting (1)
  4:16
redundancy (1)
  5:19
refused (2)
  9:16;14:10
regarding (2)
  12:3,18
Regional (3)
  6:18,19;7:19
regretted (1)
  14:8
regular (1)
  9:6
regularly (1)
  8:17
reinventing (1)
  10:13
remember (2)
  6:24;11:22
REMEMBERED (1)
  2:3
Reporter (2)
  2:8,14
Reporters (1)
  2:5
request (1)
  9:22

respect (2)
  10:20,21
respected (2)
  10:19;14:15
response (1)
  12:21
responsibilities (1)
  3:13
responsibility (1)
  3:17
retention (1)
  3:17
revenues (1)
  5:4
rework (1)
  6:11
right (4)
  4:15;5:10;8:14;
  13:22
rolled (1)
  9:10
Rome (1)
  8:10
room (1)
  14:16
rose (1)
  13:21
run (2)
  3:11;14:4

S

sales (9)
  6:1,18,19;7:3;8:13,
  20;9:2;10:6;11:4
salesperson (1)
  9:25
salts (1)
  7:22
SAN (3)
  2:1,6,8
Sassower (2)
  8:16;12:16
Sauganash (1)
  2:22
saw (1)
  5:19
scenes (2)
  7:24;11:10
School (3)
  4:12,15;10:24
screen (1)
  4:22
sector (1)
  4:20
seeing (1)
  6:13
seemed (1)
  5:4
sell (1)
  3:15
selling (1)
  9:16

seminars (1)
  9:6
send (2)
  11:17,23
sense (1)
  7:3
sent (1)
  7:18
set (2)
  8:3,24
several (1)
  5:12
shame (1)
  14:11
Sharon (8)
  6:16,17,23;9:19;
  10:16;11:24;12:18;
  13:24
Shorthand (2)
  2:8,14
show (1)
  3:11
Simply (1)
  9:13
situation (1)
  14:13
six (1)
  3:4
social (4)
  8:14,15;9:8,14
sold (1)
  10:14
solid (2)
  4:8;5:3
sometimes (1)
  8:6
somewhere (1)
  6:15
sort (1)
  4:10
spare (1)
  13:1
sparked (1)
  5:2
speak (1)
  12:18
specific (1)
  12:15
spectacular (1)
  10:7
spinning (1)
  5:25
spoke (1)
  5:7
staff (4)
  5:5,19;8:13;9:3
standard (1)
  12:12
Stanford (1)
  4:12
start (3)
  4:1;6:15;8:17
started (4)

4:3;6:13;7:25;13:17
State (2)
  2:9,18
stayed (1)
  11:5
steady (1)
  11:5
still (1)
  5:25
stores (1)
  11:6
Stormed (1)
  14:18
Strategies (2)
  4:4;7:17
strategy (2)
  3:14;11:8
Street (2)
  2:6,22
strong (3)
  4:16;5:3;10:6
struggle (1)
  12:10
stubborn (1)
  8:2
stuck (1)
  9:15
studied (1)
  4:8
studying (1)
  4:20
stuff (1)
  12:12
suggested (1)
  7:17
suggestions (2)
  9:20;10:1
Suite (1)
  2:6
sullen (1)
  14:21
superiors (1)
  5:24
supervisor (1)
  9:22
supervisors (1)
  5:8
Sure (3)
  4:24;10:12;11:4
surprised (1)
  13:6
surprising (1)
  13:9
sworn (1)
  2:13

T

talent (1)
  13:21
talented (1)
  9:25
target (1)

SHARON WATSON vs.		**DANIELLE ERIN KHOURI**
CENTURY TECHNOLOGIES, INC.		**October 7, YR-1**

8:24
teach (2)
  9:2,5
tech (1)
  6:1
Technologies (1)
  3:8
technology (1)
  4:20
tells (1)
  7:12
testified (1)
  2:15
thereof (1)
  2:5
third (1)
  3:20
though (1)
  10:19
thought (1)
  11:25
three (1)
  4:25
thrived (1)
  9:11
times (1)
  9:1
tiptoed (1)
  11:9
title (1)
  6:10
Told (3)
  14:3,7,14
took (2)
  5:24;8:12
total (1)
  5:20
tough (1)
  9:4
training (1)
  8:17
transfer (2)
  12:19,25
tricks (1)
  9:5
tried (3)
  4:8;9:6;11:10
trimming (1)
  6:15
truth (3)
  2:14,15,15
trying (1)
  9:17
two (1)
  4:25

U

ultimately (1)
  6:3
underperforming (1)
  4:21
unwillingness (1)

5:20
up (5)
  4:18;6:3;7:13;8:16;
  13:21
upset (1)
  9:23

V

vets (1)
  11:14
vice (2)
  5:14;6:9
voice (1)
  3:18
VP (1)
  11:9

W

waltzes (1)
  7:12
Watson (4)
  6:16;9:19;10:16;
  11:24
way (1)
  14:20
ways (2)
  8:3;9:15
web (1)
  11:7
weight (2)
  8:1,7
weren't (4)
  5:4;7:23;9:16;10:7
wheel (1)
  10:14
whole (1)
  2:14
willing (2)
  7:7;10:24
without (1)
  10:1
Witness (2)
  2:12,12
world (1)
  11:12
wrong (1)
  12:6

Y

year (1)
  14:22
years (3)
  3:4;4:25;8:2
Year's (1)
  11:2
yelling (2)
  13:17;14:10
young (2)
  10:23;11:19
younger (4)

9:7;12:3,8,11
Yourworld (3)
  8:15,18;10:4
Yourworlding (2)
  8:20,22

1

11:30 (1)
  2:5

2

2002 (1)
  13:19
2003 (1)
  11:2
2004 (2)
  4:24;10:11
2009 (3)
  6:6,21,22
201 (1)
  2:5
2013 (2)
  2:1,4
27-year-old (1)
  7:12

3

375 (1)
  2:6

7

7 (1)
  2:1
724 (1)
  2:22
7th (1)
  2:3

Min-U-Script®   **Barkley Court Reporters**

U.S. DISTRICT COURT
FOR THE STATE OF NITA

Civil Division

SHARON WATSON,	)	
	)	
Plaintiff,	)	CAL: 2011-CIV-10886
v.	)	
	)	Errata to Deposition of
CENTURY TECHNOLOGIES, INC.,	)	Danielle Khouri
	)	
Defendant.	)	

CORRECTIONS AND CHANGES TO DEPOSITION TRANSCRIPT OF DANIELLE KHOURI

I have read the foregoing deposition transcript and by signing here I approve the same with the following correction.

PAGE(S)	LINE	CHANGE	REASON
10	9	Delete "certificate" and insert "territory"	clarification

December 1, YR-1
Date

Danielle Khouri
Danielle Khouri

Aaron Sassower

Page 1!

```
 1        IN THE UNITED STATES DISTRICT COURT FOR
 2      THE DISTRICT OF NITA CITY, NITA
 3              CIVIL DIVISION
 4              ---oOo---
 5
 6
 7
 8      SHARON WATSON 6232 N. Ionia    )
        Avenue, Nita City, Nita,       )
 9                                     )
        Plaintiff,        )Case No. CAL:
10                                     )2011-CIV-10886
        vs.                            )
11                                     )
        CENTURY TECHNOLOGIES,  INC.,   )
12      32  W.  Dearborn  Street,  Nita)
        City,    Nita,                 )
13                                     )
        Defendant.         )
14                                     )
15
16
17
18              ---oOo---
18      MONDAY, OCTOBER 7, YR-1
19
20      DEPOSITION OF AARON SASSOWER
21              ---oOo---
22
23
24
25  REPORTER: BALINDA DUNLAP, CSR 10710, RPR, CRR, RMR
```

Page 2

```
 1      NITA CITY, NITA, OCTOBER 7,YR-1
 2              ---oOo---
 3      BE IT REMEMBERED that on Monday, the 7th
 4  day of October YR-1, commencing at the hour of 9:30
 5  a.m. thereof, at Barkley Court Reporters, 201
 6  California Street, Suite 375, Nita City,
 7  Nita, before me, Balinda Dunlap, a Certified
 8  Shorthand Reporter in and for County of Nita
 9  State of Nita, personally
10  appeared:
11              AARON SASSOWER
12      a Witness herein; called as a witness; who,
13  after having been duly sworn by the Certified
14  Shorthand Reporter to tell the truth, the whole
15  truth, and nothing but the truth, testified as
16  follows:
17              ---oOo---
18  Q.  Please state your name for the record.
19  A.  Aaron Michael Sassower.
20  Q.  What is your current address?
21  A.  1642 N. Greenview Street, Nita City,
22  Nita.
23  Q.  Do you live alone?
24  A.  No, I live with a few roommates.
25  Q.  How many?
```

Page 3

```
 1  A.  It is myself and three other guys.
 2  Q. How do you know these gentlemen?
 3  A.  I work with one of them, Zach, and
 4  other two are friends from college.
 5  Q.  Where did you attend college?
 6  A.  I went to University of Michigan.
 7  Q.  What did you study there?
 8  A.  I was a philosophy major, and I minored in
 9  computer science.
10  Q.  When did you graduate?
11  A.  The spring of YR-12.
12  Q.  What is your current occupation?
13  A.  I am a Director of Sales for the Nita
14  City Region at Century Technologies.
15  Q.  How long have you been in that position?
16  A.  A little less than six months.
17  Q.  What position did you hold before Sales
18  Director?
19  A.  I was an Associate Analyst for New Media
20  at Century.
21  Q.  How did you come to work at Century
22  Technology?
23  A.  They were recruiting at my business
24  school.
25  Q.  Where did you go to business school?
```

Page 4

```
 1  A.  Nita College.
 2  Q.  What did you study?
 3  A.  I focused mainly on marketing,
 4  specifically on social media.
 5  Q.  What classes did you attend?
 6  A.  I don't remember all of them.  A lot of
 7  standard business school classes, like Accounting
 8  101 and things like that.  But I focused on
 9  computer technology and business relations.
10  Q.  Did you take classes in sales?
11  A.  No.
12  Q.  Did you take advanced accounting classes?
13  A.  No.
14  Q.  What were your initial responsibilities at
15  Century?
16  A.  I was brought in to completely revamp the
17  company's web presence.
18  Q.  What was wrong with the company's web
19  presence?
20  A.  It didn't exist.
21  Q.  They had no website?  No --
22  A.  Let me rephrase.  There was a website, but
23  it was terrible.  It was basically a Word document.
24  Q.  So what changes did you implement?
25  A.  Well, when I arrived in YR-7, the Board
```

Page 5

1 and some of the old-timers at Century were
2 clueless. We had to revamp the entire website's
3 interface first and foremost.
4 Q. What do you mean by "interface"?
5 A. The interface is what the viewer sees and
6 how the customer interacts with the site. Ours was just
7 awful. You literally just had a long list of people,
8 things, services. A mess.
9 Q. How did you change it?
10 A. A lot of it was stylistic. The interface just
11 made the site look better.
12 Q. What other changes did you make?
13 A. We wanted everything to be easier for our
14 long-term customers. They got their own profiles,
15 which remembered what they purchased last time. We
16 created customer rewards through the web. It was
17 great.
18 Q. How did the sales staff adjust?
19 A. They were annoyed, and actually told me
20 they lost customers because of frustration with the site,
21 but you've got to break some eggs to make an omelet.
22 Q. Did you address their concerns?
23 A. I helped them figure out the site, but I
24 didn't change my strategy.
25

Page 7

1 A. It was like teaching a little kid to ride
2 a bike. The wholesales staff came up selling
3 beepers and PCs, but was surprisingly behind the
4 curve on web stuff.
5 Q. How did they respond to the training
6 sessions?
7 A. Some were stubborn, others were really
8 enthusiastic. It depended.
9 Q. In what ways were they stubborn?
10 A. I got a lot of "I've been doing this for
11 10, 20, 30 years. I don't need to Tweet my
12 customers." Just pretty standard griping.
13 Q. Do you remember which employees made these
14 comments?
15 A. At the first meetings, for the first year
16 or so, it was a few regulars. I remember Dan
17 Castrigano, Jill Pallotta, a few others.
18 Q. Do you remember specific comments?
19 A. Everyone got bent out of shape when I made
20 a dinosaur joke in one presentation. That was one
21 of my first.
22 Q. When was that?
23 A. May YR-6, I think. I can't remember
24 exactly.
25 Q. Any other complaints?

Page 6

1 Q. What other changes did you make?
2 A. My main initiative was using social media
3 to expand our client base.
4 Q. How did you do that?
5 A. A good deal of teaching old dogs new
6 tricks. Most of our sales staff weren't even on
7 Facebook, so it was a challenge.
8 Q. What was the education process like?
9 A. Annoying, but ultimately people caught on.
10 Eventually, we had almost the entire sales staff
11 using Facebook to spread the word about Century.
12 Q. What did you do to educate people?
13 A. We held regular meetings and training
14 sessions on the proper ways to use social media.
15 Q. How many?
16 A. Once every few weeks once we got out
17 strategy in place.
18 Q. When was that?
19 A. I got there in May YR-7, so by early YR-6
20 we were doing regular strategy meetings.
21 Q. What did they entail?
22 A. They were lighthearted, but informative.
23 We wanted to make this fun for the employees
24 learning new skills.
25 Q. What kinds of materials did you present?

Page 8

1 A. During the meetings, Dan and others would
2 say, "You're alienating our longtime clients by
3 forcing us to branch out." He said he would be
4 losing people.
5 Q. Was that the case?
6 A. There were, of course, a few clients who
7 were annoyed they weren't getting the personal
8 attention they were used to. There were fewer golf
9 outings, dinners, drinks -- the old way of doing
10 things.
11 Q. How did that translate in sales?
12 A. I am not sure. I was on the media side.
13 I think we took a hit for a while, but things
14 improved to where they once were.
15 Q. How did the sales rumors you were hearing
16 change your strategy?
17 A. It didn't. The Board and upper management
18 had a vision. They said, "Do this." So I did.
19 Q. How was the personnel changing at Century
20 over this period.
21 A. It was getting younger, fresher blood in
22 every day.
23 Q. Were people being let go?
24 A. It was mainly expansion and hiring new
25 people that were right out of college or business

Page 9

1 school.
2 Q. How did they respond to the training?
3 A. What training? They were all on board
4 with social media, and they adopted really well to
5 the strategies we emphasized.
6 Q. How long were you an Associate Analyst?
7 A. Not long, but YR-5 I was promoted to
8 Director of New Media.
9 Q. Do you remember encounters with Sharon
10 Watson?
11 A. I worked with Sharon often. Her sales
12 division was our behemoth.
13 Q. What do you mean?
14 A. The Nita Region always had really strong
15 sales, but they were traditional. So I worked
16 with her a lot to get on board with our
17 strategy.
18 Q. How did she respond to the new strategy?
19 A. Better than some others, but still
20 resistant to change.
21 Q. In what ways?
22 A. Just stubborn, that's all. She said, "I
23 know my customers. I know my team. Check the
24 numbers."
25 Q. Do you recall a conversation with her on

Page 10

1 February 19, YR-2?
2 A. Yes, I do.
3 Q. Can you describe the substance of that
4 conversation?
5 A. Sharon told me after a training session on
6 using Twitter, to communicate with promotional
7 deals that the company had lost its way.
8 Q. Did she explain that?
9 A. I asked if it was her place to determine
10 the company's way, and she got angry. She went
11 through the standard, "I've been here over 20
12 years, and I know how to sell."
13 Q. How did you respond?
14 A. I told her my directions were coming from
15 up high, and she should get with the program.
16 Q. How did she respond?
17 A. She left, mumbled something, who knows
18 what, under her breath. She emailed me later, but
19 I didn't respond.
20 Q. Why not?
21 A. I had nothing to add to our conversation,
22 and figured she was just blowing off steam.
23 Q. Did you have any other incidents with
24 Sharon?
25 A. Yeah, a few times she went to Jim Stancil

Page 11

1 at HR. She had a hard time handling jokes.
2 Q. What kind of jokes?
3 A. Just lighthearted ribbing about the
4 Internet changes we were going through. A few
5 funny comments in training sessions.
6 Q. How did she handle it?
7 A. Well, the worst part was that she went to
8 Stancil and Danielle. There was no reason to blow
9 it so out of proportion.
10 Q. How did Danielle react?
11 A. She told me to be respectful, and I
12 explained I was just kidding around. She said she
13 knew, and I should keep pushing people to get on
14 the right page.
15 Q. What about the birthday card in November
16 YR-3?
17 A. That was just ludicrous. It was a silly
18 joke, and Sharon blew it completely out of
19 proportion.
20 Q. How did you react?
21 A. That was kind of the last straw. After
22 that, I knew Sharon wasn't someone to be a friend,
23 just a coworker.
24 Q. Can you recall when Sharon was terminated?
25 A. Yes. It was in May YR-2.

Page 12

1 Q. Were you involved in the decision to
2 terminate her?
3 A. Of course not; that's wasn't my place.
4 Q. How were you informed?
5 A. When Danielle told me I was taking her
6 position heading up sales for Nita.
7 Q. Why were you selected?
8 A. Because I'm qualified, and loyal to
9 Danielle, and unlike some others around here, I
10 bought into the system. I believe in it.
11 Q. And Sharon did not?
12 A. She was stuck in her old ways and just
13 wouldn't change to meet a changing world. It was
14 her own fault.
15 Q. How have your sales been?
16 A. Up and down, not great, but Sharon was
17 always a solid saleswoman. Some of her clients
18 were furious she was sacked.
19 Q. How do you know?
20 A. Because they became my clients and called
21 me to say they were furious. I explained we had a
22 new mindset at the company. They had none of it.
23 Q. Which customers did you lose?
24 A. A few of the blue chips. We lost Markey
25 Industrial; they were a huge account. We also lost

Page 13

1   Amalgamated Pharmaceuticals; they were not happy.

2   Q. What did they say?

3   A. I spoke with Xavier McDermott at AmPharm,

4   and he asked to speak to the new sales director. I

5   told him I was, and he laughed.

6   Q. Why?

7   A. He told me he was tired of working with

8   toddlers, and that Century was turning into a day

9   care center.

10 Q. How did you feel about that?

11 A. For every good old boy who hates us

12 whipper snappers, there are five new start-ups that

13 give us their business. It doesn't bother me.

14 Q. Have you spoken to Sharon since she was

15 terminated?

16 A. No, not since Danielle told me to keep

17 quiet.

18 Q. Why did she tell you to keep quiet?

19 A. Not quiet, I mean not to speak with Sharon

20 since the lawyers expected her to start this silly

21 lawsuit process any time now. It's not unusual.

22 Q. Have there been any changes since Sharon

23 was terminated?

24 A. We had a new mandatory sensitivity

25 training for respect in the workplace.

Page 14

1   Q. Did you attend?

2   A. Everyone did.

3   Q. Did you find it helpful?

4   A. I mean, I try to be respectful of

5   everyone. So I felt like it was a waste of time.

6

7

8

9

10

11

12

13

14

15

16

17

18

19

20

21

22

23

24

25

Page 15

1   DEPOSITION OFFICER'S CERTIFICATE

2   STATE OF NITA   )

3   COUNTY OF NITA   ) ss.
)

4

5

6   I, Balinda Dunlap, hereby certify:

7   I am a duly qualified Certified Shorthand

8   Reporter in the State of Nita, holder of

9   Certificate Number CSR 10710 issued by the Court

10 Reporters Board of Nita and which is in full force

11 and effect. (Fed. R. Civ. P. 28(a)).

12   I am authorized to administer oaths or

13 affirmations pursuant to Nita Code of Civil

14 Procedure, Section 2093(b) and prior to being examined,

15 the witness was first duly sworn by me. (Fed. R. Civ.

16 P. 28(a), 30(f)(1)).

17   I am not a relative or employee or attorney or

18 counsel of any of the parties, nor am I a relative or

19 employee of such attorney or counsel, nor am I

20 financially interested in this action. (Fed. R. Civ. P.

21 28).

22   I am the deposition officer that

23 stenographically recorded the testimony in the foregoing

24 deposition and the foregoing transcript is a true record

25   / / /

Page 16

1   of the testimony given by the witness. (Fed. R. Civ. P.

2   30(f)(1)).

3   Before completion of the deposition, review of

4   the transcript [ ] was [ ] was not requested. If

5   requested, any changes made by the deponent (and

6   provided to the reporter) during the period allowed, are

7   appended hereto. (Fed. R. Civ. P. 30(e)).

8

9   Dated: October 21, YR-1

10

11

12   _____

13

14

15

16

17

18

19

20

21

22

23

24

25

SHARON WATSON vs.
CENTURY TECHNOLOGIES, INC.

AARON SASSOWER
October 7, YR-1

A

AARON (2)
2:11,19
account (1)
12:25
accounting (2)
4:7,12
actually (1)
5:19
add (1)
10:21
address (2)
2:20;5:23
adjust (1)
5:18
adopted (1)
9:4
advanced (1)
4:12
alienating (1)
8:2
almost (1)
6:10
alone (1)
2:23
always (2)
9:14;12:17
Amalgamated (1)
13:1
AmPharm (1)
13:3
Analyst (2)
3:19;9:6
angry (1)
10:10
annoyed (2)
5:19;8:7
Annoying (1)
6:9
appeared (1)
2:10
around (2)
11:12;12:9
arrived (1)
4:25
Associate (2)
3:19;9:6
attend (3)
3:5;4:5;14:1
attention (1)
8:8
awful (1)
5:7

B

Balinda (1)
2:7
Barkley (1)
2:5
base (1)

6:3
basically (1)
4:23
became (1)
12:20
beepers (1)
7:3
behemoth (1)
9:12
behind (1)
7:3
bent (1)
7:19
better (2)
5:11;9:19
bike (1)
7:2
birthday (1)
11:15
blew (1)
11:18
blood (1)
8:21
blow (1)
11:8
blowing (1)
10:22
blue (1)
12:24
Board (4)
4:25;8:17;9:3,16
bother (1)
13:13
bought (1)
12:10
boy (1)
13:11
branch (1)
8:3
break (1)
5:21
breath (1)
10:18
brought (1)
4:16
business (6)
3:23,25;4:7,9;8:25;
13:13

C

CALIFORNIA (4)
2:1,6,7,9
called (2)
2:12;12:20
came (1)
7:2
Can (2)
10:3;11:24
card (1)
11:15
care (1)
13:9

case (1)
8:5
Castrigano (1)
7:17
caught (1)
6:9
center (1)
13:9
Century (8)
3:14,20,21;4:15;5:1;
6:11;8:19;13:8
Certified (2)
2:7,13
challenge (1)
6:7
change (5)
5:9,25;8:16;9:20;
12:13
changes (5)
4:24;5:12;6:1;11:4;
13:22
changing (2)
8:19;12:13
Chatter (1)
10:6
Check (1)
9:23
chips (1)
12:24
classes (4)
4:5,7,10,12
client (1)
6:3
clients (4)
8:2,6;12:17,20
clueless (1)
5:2
college (4)
3:4,5;4:1;8:25
Columbia (5)
2:22;3:14;4:1;9:14;
12:6
coming (1)
10:14
commencing (1)
2:4
comments (3)
7:14,18;11:5
communicate (1)
10:6
company (2)
10:7;12:22
company's (3)
4:17,18;10:10
complaints (1)
7:25
completely (2)
4:16;11:18
computer (2)
3:9;4:9
concerns (1)
5:23
conversation (3)

9:25;10:4,21
County (1)
2:8
course (2)
8:6;12:3
Court (1)
2:5
coworker (1)
11:23
create (1)
5:16
current (2)
2:20;3:12
curve (1)
7:4
customer (2)
5:6,16
customers (5)
5:14,20;7:12;9:23;
12:23

D

Dan (2)
7:16;8:1
Danielle (5)
11:8,10;12:5,9;13:16
day (3)
2:4;8:22;13:8
deal (1)
6:5
deals (1)
10:7
decision (1)
12:1
depended (1)
7:8
describe (1)
10:3
determine (1)
10:9
dinners (1)
8:9
dinosaur (1)
7:20
directions (1)
10:14
Director (4)
3:13,18;9:8;13:4
division (1)
9:12
document (1)
4:23
dogs (1)
6:5
down (1)
12:16
drinks (1)
8:9
duly (1)
2:13
Dunlap (1)
2:7

During (1)
8:1

E

early (1)
6:19
easier (1)
5:13
educate (1)
6:12
education (1)
6:8
eggs (1)
5:21
emailed (1)
10:18
emphasized (1)
9:5
employees (2)
6:23;7:13
encounters (1)
9:9
entail (1)
6:21
enthusiastic (1)
7:8
entire (2)
5:2;6:10
even (1)
6:6
Eventually (1)
6:10
Everyone (3)
7:19;14:2,5
exactly (1)
7:24
exist (1)
4:20
expand (1)
6:3
expansion (1)
8:24
expected (1)
13:20
explain (1)
10:8
explained (2)
11:12;12:21

F

fault (1)
12:14
February (1)
10:1
feel (1)
13:10
felt (1)
14:5
few (8)
2:24;6:16;7:16,17;
8:6;10:25;11:4;12:24

Barkley Court Reporters

fewer (1)
8:8
figure (1)
5:24
figured (1)
10:22
find (1)
14:3
first (4)
5:3;7:15,15,21
five (1)
13:12
focused (2)
4:3,8
follows (1)
2:16
forcing (1)
8:3
foremost (1)
5:3
FRANCISCO (3)
2:1,6,9
fresher (1)
8:21
friend (1)
11:22
friends (1)
3:4
frustration (1)
5:20
fun (1)
6:23
funny (1)
11:5
furious (2)
12:18,21

G

gentlemen (1)
3:2
golf (1)
8:8
good (2)
6:5;13:11
graduate (1)
3:10
great (2)
5:17;12:16
Greenview (1)
2:21
griping (1)
7:12
guys (1)
3:1

H

handle (1)
11:6
handling (1)
11:1
happy (1)

13:1
hard (1)
11:1
hates (1)
13:11
heading (1)
12:6
hearing (1)
8:15
held (1)
6:13
helped (1)
5:24
helpful (1)
14:3
herein (1)
2:12
high (1)
10:15
hiring (1)
8:24
hit (1)
8:13
hold (1)
3:17
hour (1)
2:4
HR (1)
11:1
huge (1)
12:25

I

implement (1)
4:24
improved (1)
8:14
incidents (1)
10:23
Industrial (1)
12:25
informative (1)
6:22
informed (1)
12:4
initial (1)
4:14
initiative (1)
6:2
interacts (1)
5:6
interface (4)
5:3,4,5,10
Internet (1)
11:4
into (2)
12:10;13:8
involved (1)
12:1

J

Jill (1)
7:17
Jim (1)
10:25
joke (2)
7:20;11:18
jokes (2)
11:1,2

K

keep (3)
11:13;13:16,18
kid (1)
7:1
kidding (1)
11:12
kind (2)
11:2,21
kinds (1)
6:25
knew (2)
11:13,22
knows (1)
10:17

L

last (2)
5:15;11:21
later (1)
10:18
laughed (1)
13:5
lawsuit (1)
13:21
lawyers (1)
13:20
learning (1)
6:24
left (1)
10:17
less (1)
3:16
lighthearted (2)
6:22;11:3
list (1)
5:7
literally (1)
5:7
little (2)
3:16;7:1
live (2)
2:23,24
long (4)
3:15;5:7;9:6,7
long-term (1)
5:14
longtime (1)
8:2
look (1)
5:11
lose (1)

12:23
losing (1)
8:4
lost (4)
5:20;10:7;12:24,25
lot (4)
4:6;5:10;7:10;9:16
loyal (1)
12:8
ludicrous (1)
11:17

M

main (1)
6:2
mainly (2)
4:3;8:24
major (1)
3:8
management (1)
8:17
mandatory (1)
13:24
many (2)
2:25;6:15
marketing (1)
4:3
Markey (1)
12:24
materials (1)
6:25
May (3)
6:19;7:23;11:25
McDermott (1)
13:3
mean (4)
5:4;9:13;13:19;14:4
Media (7)
3:19;4:4;6:2,14;
8:12;9:4,8
meet (1)
12:13
meetings (4)
6:13,20;7:15;8:1
mess (1)
5:8
Michael (1)
2:19
Michigan (1)
3:6
mindset (1)
12:22
minored (1)
3:8
Monday (1)
2:3
months (1)
3:16
Most (1)
6:6
mumbled (1)
10:17

myself (1)
3:1

N

name (1)
2:18
need (1)
7:11
New (15)
2:21;3:13,19;4:1;6:5,
24;8:24;9:8,14,18;
12:6,22;13:4,12,24
none (1)
12:22
November (1)
11:15
numbers (1)
9:24

O

o0o- (2)
2:2,17
occupation (1)
3:12
OCTOBER (2)
2:1,4
off (1)
10:22
often (1)
9:11
old (4)
6:5;8:9;12:12;13:11
old-timers (1)
5:1
omelet (1)
5:22
Once (3)
6:16,16;8:14
one (3)
3:3;7:20,20
others (5)
7:7,17;8:1;9:19;12:9
Ours (1)
5:6
out (7)
5:24;6:16;7:19;8:3,
25;11:9,18
outings (1)
8:9
over (2)
8:20;10:11
own (2)
5:14;12:14

P

page (1)
11:14
Pallotta (1)
7:17
part (1)

11:7
PCs (1)
7:3
people (7)
5:8;6:9,12;8:4,23,25;
11:13
period (1)
8:20
personal (1)
8:7
personally (1)
2:9
personnel (1)
8:19
Pharmaceuticals (1)
13:1
philosophy (1)
3:8
place (3)
6:17;10:9;12:3
Please (1)
2:18
position (3)
3:15,17;12:6
presence (2)
4:17,19
present (1)
6:25
presentation (1)
7:20
pretty (1)
7:12
process (2)
6:8;13:21
profiles (1)
5:14
program (1)
10:15
promoted (1)
9:7
promotional (1)
10:6
proper (1)
6:14
proportion (2)
11:9,19
purchased (1)
5:15
pushing (1)
11:13

Q

qualified (1)
12:8
quiet (3)
13:17,18,19

R

react (2)
11:10,20
really (3)

7:7;9:4,14
reason (1)
11:8
recall (2)
9:25;11:24
record (1)
2:18
recruiting (1)
3:23
Region (2)
3:14;9:14
regular (2)
6:13,20
regulars (1)
7:16
relations (1)
4:9
remember (6)
4:6;7:13,16,18,23;
9:9
REMEMBERED (2)
2:3;5:15
rephrase (1)
4:22
Reporter (2)
2:8,14
Reporters (1)
2:5
resistant (1)
9:20
respect (1)
13:25
respectful (2)
11:11;14:4
respond (6)
7:5;9:2,18;10:13,16,
19
responsibilities (1)
4:14
revamp (2)
4:16;5:2
ribbing (1)
11:3
ride (1)
7:1
right (2)
8:25;11:14
roommates (1)
2:24
rumors (1)
8:15

S

sacked (1)
12:18
Sales (13)
3:13,17;4:10;5:18;
6:6,10;8:11,15;9:11,
15;12:6,15;13:4
saleswoman (1)
12:17
SAN (3)

2:1,6,8
SASSOWER (2)
2:11,19
Sauganash (1)
2:21
school (4)
3:24,25;4:7;9:1
science (1)
3:9
sees (1)
5:5
selected (1)
12:7
sell (1)
10:12
selling (1)
7:2
sensitivity (1)
13:24
services (1)
5:8
session (1)
10:5
sessions (3)
6:14;7:6;11:5
shape (1)
7:19
Sharon (12)
9:9,11;10:5,24;
11:18,22,24;12:11,16;
13:14,19,22
Shorthand (2)
2:8,14
side (1)
8:12
silly (2)
11:17;13:20
site (4)
5:6,11,21,24
six (1)
3:16
skills (1)
6:24
snappers (1)
13:12
social (4)
4:4;6:2,14;9:4
solid (1)
12:17
someone (1)
11:22
speak (2)
13:4,19
specific (1)
7:18
specifically (1)
4:4
spoke (1)
13:3
spoken (1)
13:14
spread (1)
6:11

spring (1)
3:11
staff (4)
5:18;6:6,10;7:2
Stancil (2)
10:25;11:8
standard (3)
4:7;7:12;10:11
start (1)
13:20
start-ups (1)
13:12
State (2)
2:9,18
steam (1)
10:22
still (1)
9:19
strategies (1)
9:5
strategy (6)
5:25;6:17,20;8:16;
9:17,18
straw (1)
11:21
Street (2)
2:6,21
strong (1)
9:15
stubborn (3)
7:7,9;9:22
stuck (1)
12:12
study (2)
3:7;4:2
stuff (1)
7:4
stylistic (1)
5:10
substance (1)
10:3
Suite (1)
2:6
sure (1)
8:12
surprisingly (1)
7:3
sworn (1)
2:13
system (1)
12:10

T

teaching (2)
6:5;7:1
team (1)
9:23
Technologies (1)
3:14
Technology (2)
3:22;4:9
terminate (1)

12:2
terminated (3)
11:24;13:15,23
terrible (1)
4:23
testified (1)
2:15
thereof (1)
2:5
three (1)
3:1
times (1)
10:25
tired (1)
13:7
toddlers (1)
13:8
told (8)
5:19;10:5,14;11:11;
12:5;13:5,7,16
took (1)
8:13
traditional (1)
9:15
training (7)
6:13;7:5;9:2,3;10:5;
11:5;13:25
translate (1)
8:11
tricks (1)
6:6
truth (3)
2:14,15,15
try (1)
14:4
turning (1)
13:8
Tweet (1)
7:11
two (1)
3:4

U

ultimately (1)
6:9
under (1)
10:18
University (1)
3:6
unlike (1)
12:9
unusual (1)
13:21
up (4)
7:2;10:15;12:6,16
upper (1)
8:17
use (1)
6:14
used (1)
8:8
using (3)

6:2,11;10:6

V

---

viewer (1)
5:5
vision (1)
8:18

W

---

wards (1)
5:16
waste (1)
14:5
Watson (1)
9:10
way (3)
8:9;10:7,10
ways (4)
6:14;7:9;9:21;12:12
web (4)
4:17,18;5:16;7:4
website (2)
4:21,22
website's (1)
5:2
weeks (1)
6:16
weren't (2)
6:6;8:7
whipper (1)
13:12
whole (1)
2:14
wholesales (1)
7:2
Witness (2)
2:12,12
Word (2)
4:23;6:11
work (2)
3:3,21
worked (2)
9:11,16
working (1)
13:7
workplace (1)
13:25
world (1)
12:13
worst (1)
11:7
wrong (1)
4:18

X

Xavier (1)
13:3

Y

---

year (1)
7:15
years (2)
7:11;10:12
younger (1)
8:21

Z

Zach (1)
3:3

1

---

10 (1)
7:11
101 (1)
4:8
1642 (1)
2:21
19 (1)
10:1

2

---

20 (2)
7:11;10:11
2001 (1)
11:25
2002 (1)
10:1
2003 (1)
11:16
2005 (1)
9:7
2006 (2)
6:19;7:23
2007 (2)
4:25;6:19
201 (1)
2:5
2012 (1)
3:11
2013 (2)
2:1,4

3

---

30 (1)
7:11
375 (1)
2:6

7

---

7 (1)
2:1
7th (1)
2:3

9

9:30 (1)
2:4

Jim Stancil

undefined

Jim Stancil

Page 1

```
 1        IN THE UNITED STATES DISTRICT COURT
 2      FOR THE DISTRICT OF NITA CITY, NITA
 3                 CIVIL DIVISION
 4                  ---o0o---
 5
 6
 7   SHARON WATSON 6232 N. Ionia
 8   Avenue, Nita City, Nita
                                    )
 9                                  )
                                    )
10            Plaintiff,      )Case No. CAL:
                             )2011-CIV-10886
11      vs.                   )
                             )
12   CENTURY TECHNOLOGIES, INC., 32  )
     W. Dearborn Street, Nita City,  )
13   Nita                    )
               Defendant.    )
14                           )
15
16
17
18              ---o0o---
19        MONDAY, OCTOBER 7, YR-1
20      DEPOSITION OF JAMES MATTHEW STANCIL
21              ---o0o---
22
23
     REPORTER: BALINDA DUNLAP, CSR 10710, RPR, CRR, RMR
24
25
```

Page 2

```
 1        NITA CITY, NITA, OCTOBER 7, YR-1
 2              ---o0o---
 3        BE IT REMEMBERED that on Monday, the 7th
 4   day of October YR-1, commencing at the hour of
 5   10:30 a.m. thereof, at Barkley Court Reporters, 201
 6   California Street, Suite 375, Nita City,
 7   Nita, before me, Balinda Dunlap, a Certified
 8   Shorthand Reporter in and for the County of Nita,
 9   State of Nita, personally
10   appeared:
11        JAMES MATTHEW STANCIL
12     a Witness herein; called as a witness; who,
13   after having been duly sworn by the Certified
14   Shorthand Reporter to tell the truth, the whole
15   truth, and nothing but the truth, testified as
16   follows:
17              ---o0o---
18   Q.  What is your name?
19   A.  James Matthew Stancil.
20   Q.  Can you tell us your address?
21   A.  I live in Nita City. I'm at 4800 N.
22   Belmont Avenue in Nita City.
23   Q.  How long have you lived in Nita City?
24   A.  Most of my life. I moved here when I was
25   ten.
```

Page 3

```
 1   Q.  Did you attend college?
 2   A.  I did. I got my degree in English from
 3   University of Brunswick.
 4   Q.  What brought you back to Nita?
 5   A.  It's my home. I wanted to get established
 6   here.
 7   Q.  What was your first job after graduating?
 8   A.  I was a substitute teacher for my first
 9   few years after college. I taught high school
10   English and painted houses in my spare time.
11   Q.  When did you graduate college?
12   A.  The spring of YR-33.
13   Q.  When did you begin working for Century
14   Technologies?
15   A.  I joined in late YR-16. They were
16   expanding, and a good friend of mine said they were
17   looking for someone in Human Resources.
18   Q.  What experience did you have in HR?
19   A.  Well, I couldn't just go on painting
20   houses forever, so I took a course in Human
21   Resources at the community college. I
22   got a postgraduate certificate in HR.
23   Q.  Did you work in HR prior to joining
24   Century?
25   A.  Yes. I was the Assistant Director of HR
```

Page 4

```
 1   for a small car rental company in Nita City before
 2   Century took me on.
 3   Q.  How well did you know Sharon Watson?
 4   A.  Very well. We worked together for years,
 5   and I'd say we became close friends.
 6   Q.  How would you say she was treated by
 7   Century?
 8   A.  That's a pretty broad question. I
 9   wouldn't know where to start.
10   Q.  How was she treated immediately preceding
11   her termination?
12   A.  I mean, things were not good between
13   Sharon and Danielle. Everyone knew it.
14   Q.  How do you know everyone knew it?
15   A.  I'm the HR Director. I am the eyes and
16   ears of that office, so I knew. People would make
17   comments about it after Sharon and Danielle would
18   have at it.
19   Q.  Did you ever get involved?
20   A.  Sharon never filed a formal complaint, but
21   she would vent. It gave me a sense of how other
22   veteran employees were feeling.
23   Q.  About what did she vent?
24   A.  She felt unappreciated. Ever since
25   Danielle and others joined in YR-9 and YR-8,
```

Page 5

1 veteran sales staff and executives felt like they
2 were being ignored.
3   Q. What did she say to you about how she
4 felt?
5   A. Well, in my HR capacity, not much. But as
6 a friend, she and I would talk after work about how
7 these "young pups," as she'd call them,
8 disrespected her.
9   Q. So she never filed a formal complaint?
10   A. She brought an issue to me, but she never
11 requested a formal mediation or file a compliant.
12   Q. How does a formal mediation work?
13   A. Well, our HR protocols try to emphasize
14 working together to iron out differences. We are
15 usually pretty successful, most people get along
16 well at our office. Mediation is a conversation
17 that takes place to work things out.
18   Q. Did you have mediations with older
19 employees about their age and comments made?
20   A. Several.
21   Q. What was the nature of those mediations?
22   A. A few veterans came in to complain that
23 the newer employees would disrespect them, make fun
24 of them, tease them about their age.
25   Q. Which employees brought those complaints?

Page 6

1   A. The two that come to mind were brought by
2 Lou Aldero and Marge Plimpton.
3   Q. What did Mr. Aldero bring up in the
4 mediation?
5   A. Lou was mad because one of the new guys,
6 Ben Dooley, made some joke in a meeting about Lou's
7 computer skills.
8   Q. What kind of comment?
9   A. Ben mimicked Lou's method of typing, which
10 is kind of funny, one finger at a time. Lou's from
11 a different era. Still had good numbers, though.
12   Q. When was this confrontation?
13   A. The mediation took place on September 8,
14 YR-4.
15   Q. What was the resolution?
16   A. It was all straightened out. I made a
17 record like I always do just for formal purposes,
18 and that was that.
19   Q. Is Lou still with Century?
20   A. No. His position was eliminated, and they
21 brought in some kid from Stanford.
22   Q. What about Ms. Plimpton?
23   A. Marge had a hip surgery in January YR-3,
24 and when she came back, she saw a new hire making
25 fun of the way she was walking. Then Hunter Marten

Page 7

1 put up one of those caution signs you'd see for a
2 deer crossing; but instead of a deer, it was an old
3 lady with a cane.
4   Q. When was the mediation?
5   A. Shortly after New Year's, January 20th.
6   Q. What happened in the mediation?
7   A. It didn't go well.
8   Q. Why?
9   A. Honestly, Hunter was rude and not
10 apologetic. He told Marge to lighten up, called
11 her grandma. It was bad.
12   Q. What action did you take?
13   A. I referred it to Hunter's supervisor, and
14 he supposedly took care of it.
15   Q. Is Ms. Plimpton still with the company?
16   A. Yes. She's still in her secretary
17 position, and she's been doing much better since
18 the surgery.
19   Q. Was Lou the only person to lose his
20 position?
21   A. No. The company's been through a lot of
22 changes in the last six or seven years.
23   Q. What kind of changes?
24   A. The new leaders of the company want us to
25 be more dynamic, more present on social media, more

Page 8

1 willing to explore different revenue streams.
2   Q. How has that impacted hiring?
3   A. I see a lot more graduates from Ivy League
4 schools than ever before, and it seems like the
5 employees are a lot younger.
6   Q. Why do you think that is?
7   A. Well, I'm not in charge of hiring and
8 firing. I just keep track of it.
9   Q. Keeping track of it, what have you seen?
10   A. The company's getting younger. We've got
11 the youngest CEO in our history, and the Board
12 has decided the best way to expand is through the
13 internet.
14   Q. How have older employees adjusted to the
15 changes?
16   A. Just fine for the most part. Aside from
17 the fact that more than a few have been let go.
18   Q. Why have they been let go?
19   A. A bunch of reasons. It's different for
20 every single employee. Some were just let go
21 because their positions really weren't necessary
22 anymore. Some because they just couldn't keep up
23 with the new pace.
24   Q. How was the pace?
25   A. Well, these younger employees were living,

Page 9

1 breathing, and sleeping Century Technologies.

2 Q. Can you be more specific?

3 A. They work longer hours. Their Facebook

4 pages are just covered in promotional materials.

5 They just treat their whole lives as promotional

6 tools.

7 Q. How did the veteran employees do it

8 differently?

9 A. Many tried to keep up, but many were stuck

10 in their old ways. I saw it like this when we

11 transitioned from beepers to PCs.

12 Q. What happened then?

13 A. There were many people back then who said

14 the Internet was a fad, that no one would ever want

15 a computer for every one of their employees. They

16 stuck to their old ways until they either caught up

17 or got left behind.

18 Q. How does that compare with the changes

19 recently?

20 A. Same story, but it's faster and harsher

21 than before.

22 Q. How do you mean?

23 A. We've just been losing older employees and

24 hiring a lot younger people with less sales

25 experience, but more technology and computer

Page 10

1 engineering backgrounds.

2 Q. How have you tracked this?

3 A. Every year I make records of new hires for

4 the company. Their names, addresses, educational

5 backgrounds, hire dates, and their ages.

6 Q. Do you do the same for terminations?

7 A. Yes, of course. We need to keep track of

8 those things, and that's absolutely my job.

9 Q. How have the terminations tracked age?

10 A. I don't know, exactly. There's no direct

11 correlation, but the records definitely show that

12 we're losing more older employees than younger

13 ones.

14 Q. How old are the employees being let go?

15 A. They're not even old. When I say "old,"

16 you must think I mean nearing retirement. I'm

17 talking about people in their mid to late 40s,

18 early 50s.

19 Q. How about the senior executive?

20 A. That was the really stark contrast. Since

21 YR-11, we have promoted a lot of young go-getters.

22 Q. Has that led to a loss of more experienced

23 employees?

24 A. Yes. But not all of them have been fired.

25 Q. Specifically related to Ms. Watson, how

Page 11

1 have you been involved in her termination?

2 A. Well, like I said, she would complain to

3 me about her treatment before the firing. She

4 mentioned the birthday card they gave her, the

5 jokes in meetings, the way Danielle treated her.

6 Q. What was your reply?

7 A. I thought she was just venting, so I told

8 her to relax. Sharon could be a hothead.

9 Q. How do you mean?

10 A. Well, she's tough. She had to work hard

11 to get where she got, and so sometimes she was a

12 bit quick to react.

13 Q. Was she the subject of inappropriate

14 comments about her age?

15 A. I certainly think so, but she never filed

16 a formal complaint with me. She also never wanted

17 to do a mediation.

18 Q. Why not?

19 A. I don't know. I think she wanted to

20 settle things more directly. I know she sent

21 emails to Danielle Khouri about the comments being

22 made.

23 Q. What kind of comments did you personally

24 observe?

25 A. I saw the birthday card she got, but I

Page 12

1 wasn't present for the other comments.

2 Q. Why not?

3 A. A lot of these comments were made in sales

4 meetings, or part of innuendo.

5 Q. What advice did you give her?

6 A. When she was venting, I would tell her to

7 keep quiet and not make waves.

8 Q. Why?

9 A. I saw what happened to a lot of older

10 employees without jobs. It's tough out there right

11 now. So as her friend, I told her to relax.

12 Q. Did she listen?

13 A. Yes and no. She backed off for a while,

14 but when Mackenzie was promoted to CFO she was

15 upset.

16 Q. What did she do?

17 A. She knew it was because of her age, and I

18 agreed. I mean, Sharon had been there for years

19 and Mackenzie was brand-new. As someone

20 experienced in hiring and firing, this was bizarre.

21 Q. Did you say anything?

22 A. I'm 56 years old; you had better believe I

23 kept my mouth shut. And I told Sharon to do the

24 same, but that's not what happened.

25 Q. When did you find out she had been fired?

SHARON WATSON vs.
CENTURY TECHNOLOGIES, INC.

JAMES MATTHEW STANCIL
October 7, YR-1

Page 13

1 A. Danielle called me into her office a few
2 weeks before it happened. She told me that's the
3 route they were taking and what I thought.
4 Q. What did you say?
5 A. I kept my mouth shut. Look, I sympathize
6 with Sharon. This company means well, but they're
7 treating veteran employees like dirt. That being
8 said, I would rather not be on the receiving end of
9 it.
10 Q. Did you express any reservations to
11 Danielle?
12 A. I told her she was cutting loose so many
13 employees who had been loyal, and incredibly
14 successful, since she took over.
15 Q. What was her response?
16 A. She said she was running a business, not a
17 nursing home. That's when I let it go. I feel bad
18 for Sharon, but I have kids at home.
19 Q. What happened after Sharon was fired?
20 A. The office was shocked. A lot of people
21 were nervous there would be big downsizing if the
22 Employee of the Decade could get fired.
23 Q. Did Danielle or other executives do
24 anything to calm people's nerves?
25 A. Danielle held a big office meeting with

Page 15

1 A. Hanging in there, updating her resume.
2 Can't be easy out there.
3
4
5
6
7
8
9
10
11
12
13
14
15
16
17
18
19
20
21
22
23
24
25

Page 14

1 every employee in the office.
2 Q. What did she say?
3 A. She said that Sharon was not being a team
4 player and hadn't learned to grow in the way the
5 company wanted.
6 Q. What was the mood of the meeting?
7 A. You could hear a pin drop. The younger
8 kids just nodded their heads, smirking.
9 Q. Who was smirking?
10 A. Aaron Sassower, Hunter, some others. I
11 can't remember anyone specifically besides Aaron.
12 Q. What else did Danielle say, if anything?
13 A. She said what the company has been saying
14 for years. She explained that to grow, companies
15 had to evolve. She said something about the
16 company being a shark, and if it's not moving at
17 all times, it dies.
18 Q. What do you think she meant?
19 A. I don't know. She was the CEO. She
20 wanted her ideas to be part of the new mindset of
21 the company, but I thought it was more than
22 coincidence she fired all the veteran employees.
23 Q. Have you spoken to Sharon since then?
24 A. Yes. Like I said, she is a dear friend.
25 Q. How has she been?

Page 16

1   DEPOSITION OFFICER'S CERTIFICATE
2 STATE OF NITA   )
3 COUNTY OF NITA   ) ss.
4   )
5
6   I, Balinda Dunlap, hereby certify:
7   I am a duly qualified Certified Shorthand
8 Reporter in the State of Nita, holder of
9 Certificate Number CSR 10710 issued by the Court
10 Reporters Board of Nita and which is in full force
11 and effect. (Fed. R. Civ. P. 28(a)).
12   I am authorized to administer oaths or
13 affirmations pursuant to Nita Code of Civil
14 Procedure, Section 2093(b) and prior to being examined,
15 the witness was first duly sworn by me. (Fed. R. Civ.
16 P. 28(a), 30(f)(1)).
17   I am not a relative or employee or attorney or
18 counsel of any of the parties, nor am I a relative or
19 employee of such attorney or counsel, nor am I
20 financially interested in this action. (Fed. R. Civ. P.
21 28).
22   I am the deposition officer that
23 stenographically recorded the testimony in the foregoing
24 deposition and the foregoing transcript is a true record
25   / / /

A

Aaron (2)
14:10,11
absolutely (1)
10:8
action (1)
7:12
address (1)
2:20
addresses (1)
10:4
adjusted (1)
8:14
advice (1)
12:5
age (5)
5:19,24;10:9;11:14;
12:17
ages (1)
10:5
agreed (1)
12:18
Aldero (2)
6:2,3
along (1)
5:15
always (1)
6:17
anymore (1)
8:22
apologetic (1)
7:10
appeared (1)
2:10
Aside (1)
8:16
Assistant (1)
3:25
attend (1)
3:1
Avenue (1)
2:22

B

back (3)
3:4;6:24;9:13
backed (1)
12:13
backgrounds (2)
10:1,5
bad (2)
7:11;13:17
Balinda (1)
2:7
Barkley (1)
2:5
became (1)
4:5
beepers (1)
9:11

begin (1)
3:13
behind (1)
9:17
Belmont (1)
2:22
Ben (2)
6:6,9
besides (1)
14:11
best (1)
8:12
better (2)
7:17;12:22
big (2)
13:21,25
birthday (2)
11:4,25
bit (1)
11:12
bizarre (1)
12:20
Board (1)
8:11
brand-new (1)
12:19
breathing (1)
9:1
bring (1)
6:3
broad (1)
4:8
brought (5)
3:4;5:10,25;6:1,21
Brunswick (1)
3:3
bunch (1)
8:19
business (1)
13:16

C

CALIFORNIA (4)
2:1,6,7,9
call (1)
5:7
called (3)
2:12;7:10;13:1
calm (1)
13:24
came (2)
5:22;6:24
Can (2)
2:20;9:2
cane (1)
7:3
capacity (1)
5:5
car (1)
4:1
card (2)
11:4,25

care (1)
7:14
caught (1)
9:16
caution (1)
7:1
Century (6)
3:13,24;4:2,7;6:19;
9:1
CEO (2)
8:11;14:19
certainly (1)
11:15
certificate (1)
3:22
Certified (2)
2:7,13
CFO (1)
12:14
changes (4)
7:22,23;8:15;9:18
charge (1)
8:7
close (1)
4:5
coincidence (1)
14:22
college (4)
3:1,9,11,21
Columbia (1)
3:4
commencing (1)
2:4
comment (1)
6:8
comments (7)
4:17;5:19;11:14,21,
23;12:1,3
community (1)
3:21
companies (1)
14:14
company (9)
4:1;7:15,24;10:4;
13:6;14:5,13,16,21
company's (2)
7:21;8:10
compare (1)
9:18
complain (2)
5:22;11:2
complaint (3)
4:20;5:9;11:16
complaints (1)
5:25
compliant (1)
5:11
computer (3)
6:7;9:15,25
confrontation (1)
6:12
contrast (1)
10:20

conversation (1)
5:16
correlation (1)
10:11
County (1)
2:8
course (2)
3:20;10:7
Court (1)
2:5
covered (1)
9:4
crossing (1)
7:2
cutting (1)
13:12

D

Danielle (10)
4:13,17,25;11:5,21;
13:1,11,23,25;14:12
dates (1)
10:5
day (1)
2:4
dear (1)
14:24
Decade (1)
13:22
decided (1)
8:12
deer (2)
7:2,2
definitely (1)
10:11
degree (1)
3:2
dies (1)
14:17
differences (1)
5:14
different (3)
6:11;8:1,19
differently (1)
9:8
direct (1)
10:10
directly (1)
11:20
Director (2)
3:25;4:15
dirt (1)
13:7
disrespect (1)
5:23
disrespected (1)
5:8
Dooley (1)
6:6
downsizing (1)
13:21
drop (1)

14:7
duly (1)
2:13
Dunlap (1)
2:7
dynamic (1)
7:25

E

early (1)
10:18
ears (1)
4:16
easy (1)
15:2
educational (1)
10:4
either (1)
9:16
eliminated (1)
6:20
else (1)
14:12
emails (1)
11:21
emphasize (1)
5:13
employee (2)
8:20;14:1
employees (17)
4:22;5:19,23,25;8:5,
14,25;9:7,15,23;10:12,
14,23;12:10;13:7,13;
14:22
end (1)
13:8
engineering (1)
10:1
English (2)
3:2,10
era (1)
6:11
established (1)
3:5
even (1)
10:15
Everyone (2)
4:13,14
evolve (1)
14:15
exactly (1)
10:10
executive (2)
10:19;13:22
executives (2)
5:1;13:23
expand (1)
8:12
expanding (1)
3:16
experience (2)
3:18;9:25

experienced (2)
10:22;12:20
explained (1)
14:14
explore (1)
8:1
express (1)
13:10
eyes (1)
4:15

F

fact (1)
8:17
fad (1)
9:14
faster (1)
9:20
feel (1)
13:17
feeling (1)
4:22
felt (3)
4:24;5:1,4
few (4)
3:9;5:22;8:17;13:1
file (1)
5:11
filed (3)
4:20;5:9;11:15
find (1)
12:25
fine (1)
8:16
finger (1)
6:10
fired (5)
10:24;12:25;13:19,
22;14:22
firing (3)
8:8;11:3;12:20
first (2)
3:7,8
follows (1)
2:16
forever (1)
3:20
formal (6)
4:20;5:9,11,12;6:17;
11:16
FRANCISCO (3)
2:1,6,9
friend (4)
3:16;5:6;12:11;
14:24
friends (1)
4:5
fun (2)
5:23;6:25
funny (1)
6:10

G

gave (2)
4:21;11:4
go-getters (1)
10:21
good (3)
3:16;4:12;6:11
graduate (1)
3:11
graduates (1)
8:3
graduating (1)
3:7
grandma (1)
7:11
grow (2)
14:4,14
guys (1)
6:5

H

Hanging (1)
15:1
happened (6)
7:6;9:12;12:9,24;
13:2,19
hard (1)
11:10
harsher (1)
9:20
heads (1)
14:8
hear (1)
14:7
held (1)
13:25
herein (1)
2:12
high (1)
3:9
hip (1)
6:23
hire (2)
6:24;10:5
hires (1)
10:3
hiring (4)
8:2,7;9:24;12:20
history (1)
8:11
home (3)
3:5;13:17,18
Honestly (1)
7:9
hothead (1)
11:8
hour (1)
2:4
hours (1)
9:3

houses (2)
3:10,20
HR (7)
3:18,22,23,25;4:15;
5:5,13
Human (2)
3:17,20
Hunter (3)
6:25;7:9;14:10
hunter's (1)
7:13

I

ideas (1)
14:20
ignored (1)
5:2
immediately (1)
4:10
impacted (1)
8:2
inappropriate (1)
11:13
incredibly (1)
13:13
innuendo (1)
12:4
instead (1)
7:2
Internet (2)
8:13;9:14
into (1)
13:1
involved (2)
4:19;11:1
iron (1)
5:14
issue (1)
5:10
Ivy (1)
8:3

J

JAMES (2)
2:11,19
January (2)
6:23;7:5
job (2)
3:7;10:8
jobs (1)
12:10
joined (2)
3:15;4:25
joining (1)
3:23
joke (1)
6:6
jokes (1)
11:5

K

keep (5)
8:8,22;9:9;10:7;12:7
Keeping (1)
8:9
kept (2)
12:23;13:5
Khouri (1)
11:21
kid (1)
6:21
kids (2)
13:18;14:8
kind (4)
6:8,10;7:23;11:23
knew (4)
4:13,14,16;12:17

L

lady (1)
7:3
last (1)
7:22
late (2)
3:15;10:17
leaders (1)
7:24
League (1)
8:3
learned (1)
14:4
led (1)
10:22
left (1)
9:17
less (1)
9:24
life (1)
2:24
lighten (1)
7:10
listen (1)
12:12
live (1)
2:21
lived (1)
2:23
lives (1)
9:5
living (1)
8:25
long (1)
2:23
longer (1)
9:3
Look (1)
13:5
looking (1)
3:17
loose (1)

13:12
lose (1)
7:19
losing (2)
9:23;10:12
loss (1)
10:22
lot (8)
7:21;8:3,5;9:24;
10:21;12:3,9;13:20
Lou (4)
6:2,5,19;7:19
Lou's (3)
6:6,9,10
loyal (1)
13:13

M

Mackenzie (2)
12:14,19
mad (1)
6:5
making (1)
6:24
Many (4)
9:9,9,13;13:12
Marge (3)
6:2,23;7:10
Marten (1)
6:25
materials (1)
9:4
MATTHEW (2)
2:11,19
mean (5)
4:12;9:22;10:16;
11:9;12:18
means (1)
13:6
meant (1)
14:18
media (1)
7:25
mediation (8)
5:11,12,16;6:4,13;
7:4,6;11:17
mediations (2)
5:18,21
meeting (3)
6:6;13:25;14:6
meetings (2)
11:5;12:4
mentioned (1)
11:4
method (1)
6:9
mid (1)
10:17
mimicked (1)
6:9
mind (1)
6:1

SHARON WATSON vs.
CENTURY TECHNOLOGIES, INC.

JAMES MATTHEW STANCIL
October 7, YR-1

mindset (1)
14:20
mine (1)
3:16
Monday (1)
2:3
mood (1)
14:6
more (11)
7:25,25,25;8:3,17;
9:2,25;10:12,22;11:20;
14:21
Most (3)
2:24;5:15;8:16
mouth (2)
12:23;13:5
moved (1)
2:24
moving (1)
14:16
much (2)
5:5;7:17
must (1)
10:16

N

name (1)
2:18
names (1)
10:4
nature (1)
5:21
nearing (1)
10:16
necessary (1)
8:21
need (1)
10:7
nerves (1)
13:24
nervous (1)
13:21
New (8)
3:4;6:5,24;7:5,24;
8:23;10:3;14:20
newer (1)
5:23
nodded (1)
14:8
numbers (1)
6:11
nursing (1)
13:17

O

o0o- (2)
2:2,17
observe (1)
11:24
OCTOBER (2)
2:1,4

off (1)
12:13
office (6)
4:16;5:16;13:1,20,
25;14:1
old (7)
7:2;9:10,16;10:14,
15,15;12:22
older (5)
5:18;8:14;9:23;
10:12;12:9
one (5)
6:5,10;7:1;9:14,15
ones (1)
10:13
only (1)
7:19
others (2)
4:25;14:10
out (6)
5:14,17;6:16;12:10,
25;15:2
over (1)
13:14

P

pace (2)
8:23,24
pages (1)
9:4
painted (1)
3:10
painting (1)
3:19
part (3)
8:16;12:4;14:20
PCs (1)
9:11
People (6)
4:16;5:15;9:13,24;
10:17;13:20
people's (1)
13:24
person (1)
7:19
personally (2)
2:9;11:23
pin (1)
14:7
place (2)
5:17;6:13
player (1)
14:4
Plimpton (3)
6:2,22;7:15
position (3)
6:20;7:17,20
positions (1)
8:21
postgraduate (1)
3:22
preceding (1)

4:10
present (2)
7:25;12:1
pretty (2)
4:8;5:15
prior (1)
3:23
promoted (2)
10:21;12:14
promotional (2)
9:4,5
protocols (1)
5:13
pups (1)
5:7
purposes (1)
6:17
put (1)
7:1

Q

quick (1)
11:12
quiet (1)
12:7

R

rather (1)
13:8
react (1)
11:12
really (2)
8:21;10:20
reasons (1)
8:19
receiving (1)
13:8
recently (1)
9:19
record (1)
6:17
records (2)
10:3,11
referred (1)
7:13
related (1)
10:25
relax (2)
11:8;12:11
remember (1)
14:11
REMEMBERED (1)
2:3
rental (1)
4:1
reply (1)
11:6
Reporter (2)
2:8,14
Reporters (1)
2:5

requested (1)
5:11
reservations (1)
13:10
resolution (1)
6:15
Resources (2)
3:17,21
response (1)
13:15
resume (1)
15:1
retirement (1)
10:16
revenue (1)
8:1
right (1)
12:10
route (1)
13:3
rude (1)
7:9
running (1)
13:16

S

sales (3)
5:1;9:24;12:3
Same (3)
9:20;10:6;12:24
SAN (3)
2:1,6,8
Sassower (1)
14:10
Sauganash (4)
2:21,22,23;4:1
saw (4)
6:24;9:10;11:25;
12:9
saying (1)
14:13
school (1)
3:9
schools (1)
8:4
secretary (1)
7:16
seems (1)
8:4
senior (1)
10:19
sense (1)
4:21
sent (1)
11:20
September (1)
6:13
settle (1)
11:20
seven (1)
7:22
Several (1)

5:20
shark (1)
14:16
Sharon (12)
4:3,13,17,20;11:8;
12:18,23;13:6,18,19;
14:3,23
shocked (1)
13:20
Shorthand (2)
2:8,14
Shortly (1)
7:5
show (1)
10:11
shut (2)
12:23;13:5
signs (1)
7:1
single (1)
8:20
six (1)
7:22
skills (1)
6:7
sleeping (1)
9:1
small (1)
4:1
smirking (2)
14:8,9
social (1)
7:25
someone (2)
3:17;12:19
sometimes (1)
11:11
spare (1)
3:10
specific (1)
9:2
Specifically (2)
10:25;14:11
spoken (1)
14:23
spring (1)
3:12
staff (1)
5:1
STANCIL (2)
2:11,19
Stanford (1)
6:21
stark (1)
10:20
start (1)
4:9
State (1)
2:9
Still (4)
6:11,19;7:15,16
story (1)
9:20

SHARON WATSON vs. CENTURY TECHNOLOGIES, INC.			JAMES MATTHEW STANCIL October 7, YR-1

straightened (1)
6:16
streams (1)
8:1
Street (1)
2:6
stuck (2)
9:9,16
subject (1)
11:13
substitute (1)
3:8
successful (2)
5:15;13:14
Suite (1)
2:6
supervisor (1)
7:13
supposedly (1)
7:14
surgery (2)
6:23;7:18
sworn (1)
2:13
sympathize (1)
13:5

T

talk (1)
5:6
talking (1)
10:17
taught (1)
3:9
teacher (1)
3:8
team (1)
14:3
tease (1)
5:24
Technologies (1)
9:1
Technology (2)
3:14;9:25
ten (1)
2:25
termination (2)
4:11;11:1
terminations (2)
10:6,9
testified (1)
2:15
thereof (1)
2:5
though (1)
6:11
thought (3)
11:7;13:3;14:21
times (1)
14:17
together (2)
4:4;5:14

told (6)
7:10;11:7;12:11,23;
13:2,12
took (5)
3:20;4:2;6:13;7:14;
13:14
tools (1)
9:6
tough (2)
11:10;12:10
track (3)
8:8,9;10:7
tracked (2)
10:2,9
transitioned (1)
9:11
treat (1)
9:5
treated (3)
4:6,10;11:5
treating (1)
13:7
treatment (1)
11:3
tried (1)
9:9
truth (3)
2:14,15,15
try (1)
5:13
two (1)
6:1
typing (1)
6:9

U

unappreciated (1)
4:24
University (1)
3:3
up (6)
6:3;7:1,10;8:22;9:9,
16
updating (1)
15:1
upset (1)
12:15
usually (1)
5:15

V

vent (2)
4:21,23
venting (2)
11:7;12:6
veteran (5)
4:22;5:1;9:7;13:7;
14:22
veterans (1)
5:22

W

walking (1)
6:25
Watson (2)
4:3;10:25
waves (1)
12:7
way (4)
6:25;8:12;11:5;14:4
ways (2)
9:10,16
weeks (1)
13:2
weren't (1)
8:21
whole (2)
2:14;9:5
willing (1)
8:1
without (1)
12:10
Witness (2)
2:12,12
work (6)
3:23;5:6,12,17;9:3;
11:10
worked (1)
4:4
working (2)
3:13;5:14

Y

year (1)
10:3
years (6)
3:9;4:4;7:22;12:18,
22;14:14
Year's (1)
7:5
young (2)
5:7;10:21
younger (6)
8:5,10,25;9:24;
10:12;14:7
youngest (1)
8:11
Yourworld (1)
9:3

1

10:30 (1)
2:5
1979 (1)
3:12
1980s (1)
3:21
1990s (1)
3:15

2

2000s (1)
3:15
2002 (1)
6:23
2003 (2)
6:14;10:21
2008 (1)
4:25
2009 (1)
4:25
201 (1)
2:5
2013 (2)
2:1,4
20th (1)
7:5

3

375 (1)
2:6

4

40s (1)
10:17
4800 (1)
2:21

5

50s (1)
10:18
56 (1)
12:22

7

7 (1)
2:1
7th (1)
2:3

8

8 (1)
6:13

Sharon Watson

Page 1

```
1        IN THE UNITED STATES DISTRICT COURT
2      FOR THE DISTRICT OF NITA CITY, NITA
3                 CIVIL DIVISION
4                   ---oOo---
5
6
7
8    SHARON WATSON 6232 N. Ionia
     Avenue, Nita City, Nita,              )
9                                          )
10             Plaintiff,        )Case No. CAL:
                                 )2011-CIV-10886
11        vs.                             )
12   CENTURY TECHNOLOGIES, INC., 32        )
     W. Dearborn Street, Nita City,        )
13   Nita,                                 )
               Defendant.                  )
14                                         )
15
16
17
18                  ---oOo---
19          MONDAY, OCTOBER 7, YR-1
20       DEPOSITION OF SHARON WATSON
21                  ---oOo---
22
23
24   REPORTER: BALINDA DUNLAP, CSR 10710, RPR, CRR, RMR
25
```

Page 2

```
1        NITA CITY, NITA, OCTOBER 7, YR-1
2                   ---oOo---
3        BE IT REMEMBERED that on Monday, the 7th
4    day of October YR-1, commencing at the hour of
5    12:30 p.m. thereof, at Barkley Court Reporters, 201
6    California Street, Suite 375, Nita City,
7    Nita, before me, Balinda Dunlap, a Certified
8    Shorthand Reporter in and for the County of Nita,
9    State of Nita, personally
10   appeared:
11             SHARON WATSON
12      a Plaintiff herein; called as a witness;
13   who, after having been duly sworn by the Certified
14   Shorthand Reporter to tell the truth, the whole
15   truth, and nothing but the truth, testified as
16   follows:
17             ---oOo---
18   Q.  What is your name, ma'am?
19   A.  Sharon Watson.
20   Q.  Can you tell us your address?
21   A.  I live in Nita City.  I'm at 6232 N. Ionia
22   Avenue.
23   Q.  What is your current occupation?
24   A.  I am currently unemployed.
25   Q.  Have you been looking for work?
```

Page 3

```
1    A.  Yes, of course.  It's just not easy these
2    days.
3    Q.  In what fields are you currently looking
4    for work?
5    A.  Sales, mainly, but also marketing and
6    managerial positions.  Anything I can get my
7    hands on.
8    Q.  How old are you?
9    A.  I just turned 50.
10   Q.  Has that affected your job prospects?
11   A.  Classic double-edged sword.  Tons of
12   experience, but I'm overqualified for a lot, too.
13   Q.  When were you terminated?
14   A.  I was called into the CEO's office on May
15   19, YR-2, and told I wasn't needed anymore.
16   Q.  Why did you meet with the CEO to be
17   terminated?
18   A.  What do you mean?
19   Q.  I mean, is it usual for an employee to be
20   terminated by the CEO as opposed to a Human
21   Resources representative?
22   A.  I see.  No, it's not.  Because I was a
23   major executive, they weren't just going to send me
24   to HR with a cardboard box.
25   Q.  What was the substance of the
```

Page 4

```
1    conversation?
2    A.  I was told my services weren't needed
3    anymore.  They were going in a different direction.
4    All the usual things you hear.
5    Q.  Did they provide an explanation?
6    A.  No.  And when I asked people in the room
7    questions, I got stonewalled.  Danielle Khouri said
8    the lawyers told her not to say anything.
9    Q.  I am sorry to interrupt, but can you --
10   A.  I'm sorry, what?
11   Q.  Can you say who Danielle Khouri is in
12   relation to the company?
13   A.  Yes.  I'm sorry.  Absolutely.  Khouri is
14   now the CEO of the company, and before that she was
15   literally just a marketing guru.  She was really in
16   charge of social media presence, increasing our
17   Google ads and targeting them to customers, things
18   like that.  Then she was named CEO back in YR-3.
19   Q.  How long had you been working before being
20   unemployed?
21   A.  All my life.
22   Q.  Can you be specific?
23   A.  Gosh, I'd say well over
24   30 years.
25   Q.  Can you name your first job?
```

Page 5

1   A. Sure. Give me a second. It's been a
2   while.
3   Q. Take your time.
4   A. So I started working for Barron &
5   Associates, a law firm out in Rockpoint.
6   Q. What was your job title?
7   A. First I was a secretary answering phones.
8   Q. How did you get your job?
9   A. A family friend told me the position
10 opened up. I had a few semesters left before
11 getting my degree, but I needed to work.
12 Q. Did you finish college?
13 A. I planned on taking night classes, but the
14 money was good so I just focused on my career.
15 Q. Where was your next job?
16 A. You mean my next position or where.
17 Q. Well, let's start with position. What was
18 your next position?
19 A. I got a promotion. Well, really it was a
20 transfer to a different part of the law firm.
21 Q. What department of the firm?
22 A. I got a position in client relations. One
23 of the partners told me I had a real knack for
24 selling. He called me a natural talent, so I
25 figured I would learn something new.

Page 7

1   A. Just five of us. It was Jim Reardon, the
2   CEO; our accountant, Murray Burns; and two other
3   sales associates. I can't even remember their
4   names.
5   Q. You mentioned the company turned into a
6   monstrosity. What do you mean?
7   A. When I started, we focused on people. Now
8   it's all about the bottom line. The Almighty
9   Dollar reigns supreme.
10 Q. When would you say that changed?
11 A. Probably about 20 or so years ago.
12 Q. What happened 20 or so years ago?
13 A. Jim Reardon got bought out. A bigger
14 company that was kind of dying at the time, Beeper
15 World, was slowing down. They saw we had a good
16 client base, and they just kind of bought our
17 brand.
18 Q. Did Jim Reardon leave?
19 A. He had a kind of power-sharing deal with the
20 Beeper World executives. Jim stayed on with some
21 title, Vice President of Development or something.
22 Q. Do you remember the exact year the merger took
23 place?
24 A. It would have been sometime in the fall of,
25

Page 6

1   Q. How long were you there?
2   A. Only a few years, because another position
3   opened up at Century Technologies.
4   Q. Where did you go to college before taking
5   these jobs?
6   A. Columbia Community, in Rockpoint.
7   Q. What did you study?
8   A. A few classes in English, and I think I
9   took a pottery class. It was fun.
10 Q. What was your first position at Century?
11 A. Just your standard entry-level position.
12 I worked in sales.
13 Q. What were your responsibilities?
14 A. Basically, I was making cold calls on
15 businesses in the area, selling beepers, fax
16 machines, and those old giant cellular phones.
17 Q. What kind of businesses?
18 A. All of them. I know it sounds crazy, but
19 I felt like I called every business in the entire
20 city trying to sell them beepers.
21 Q. Were there no other salespeople?
22 A. Of course, but we were small back then.
23 Not like this giant monstrosity it's turned into
24 today.
25 Q. How many other people?

Page 8

1   uh, . . . oh, it would have been 15 or more
2   years ago.
3   Q. So do you know the date?
4   A. I don't know an exact date. It took them
5   months and months to work out the deal. Then there
6   was a transition phase, then Jim came to us and
7   said, "We're in a new direction, but keep your
8   spirits up."
9   Q. We still haven't addressed why it was a
10 monstrosity when you left. Why did you call it
11 that?
12 A. This is all part of the long process of
13 the company. By the end, everyone in the firm I
14 knew who started earlier was tired of the way they
15 treated people.
16 Q. Who were these people speaking with you
17 about this?
18 A. A lot of older sales associates. Some
19 weren't older. Some of them in their 30s, but
20 people who had been there since right after the
21 merger.
22 Q. What was the problem, as you saw it?
23 A. Like I said, it wasn't just me. Other
24 complained that the company was focused so much on
25 social media and web-based sales.

Page 9

1   Q. How did the company focus on social media?

2   A. Everything was Facebook this and Twitter

3 that. The children that took over our leadership

4 several years ago had no idea how to work with

5 customers.

6   Q. Can you be more specific?

7   A. Sure. When Danielle Khouri was just

8 another Assistant VP of Marketing or something, she

9 and some of the other spring chickens would have us

10 do these social media and new media training

11 sessions.

12   Q. What was discussed?

13   A. Danielle and others would say things like,

14 "Be the face of this company at all times," and

15 "Every new connection on Facebook is a potential

16 client."

17   Q. Do you remember who exactly led these

18 meetings?

19   A. It was Danielle and a few of her little

20 friends. Aaron Sassower was one, and Josh Hampton

21 was another.

22   Q. How long had they been with the company?

23   A. Not long at all. The Board brought them

24 in around YR-8 or YR-7; I can't remember exactly.

25   Q. Did you take their advice?

Page 10

1   A. I humored them.

2   Q. What do you mean?

3   A. I mean I did what they asked; created a

4 profile, mentioned the company now and again. I

5 did what they asked.

6   Q. What did other people do?

7   A. Some of my coworkers and subordinates went

8 crazy and just threw all kinds of stuff out on the

9 Internet. I didn't stop them. I told them I

10 wanted them to do what's best for sales and our

11 customers.

12   Q. Going back to the merger, how did the

13 company change at that point?

14   A. Mainly we changed what we were selling.

15   Q. How so?

16   A. This was right before the dot-com boom, and

17 I knew that eventually there was just no way

18 people would still be using fax machines and

19 beepers.

20   Q. How did this change the company?

21   A. We switched to selling personal computers,

22 PCs, and software. The business was just booming

23 on my end.

24   Q. What was your position at this point?

25   A. I was the Assistant Regional

Page 11

1 Director of Sales. Jim Reardon promoted me to the

2 position and told me that I saved the company with

3 my strategy.

4   Q. How did he mean?

5   A. Were you around back then? PCs

6 exploded. The internet grew into a cash cow, and

7 Century grew with the trend, thanks to me. I'll

8 never forget the first sale I made to a Fortune

9 1000 company. When I told Jim, he fell into his

10 chair and said, "Shar, you're the best thing to

11 happen to Century since the telephone cord!"

12   Q. What happened after you were promoted?

13   A. I kept climbing the ladder, making my

14 mark. They named me Employee of the Decade in YR-4.

15   Q. Did you stay in your position?

16   A. For longer than expected.

17   Q. Why was that?

18   A. There were some small accounting matters

19 that Bill accused me of, but it was taken care of

20 pretty quickly. Just a misunderstanding.

21   Q. How was it taken care of?

22   A. Bill accused me, wrongfully, of

23 appropriating funds for personal use that were

24 supposed to be for client development.

25   Q. What kind of client development?

Page 12

1   A. Dinners, drinks, sporting events. That

2 kind of thing.

3   Q. What came of that accusation?

4   A. Bill and I worked it out, but I had to

5 earn my way back to the top, which I eventually

6 did.

7   Q. Were you disciplined for this accusation?

8   A. No. Like I said, it was a

9 misunderstanding. I wasn't keeping the receipts

10 properly, and it led to a blowup, but I was never

11 formally disciplined.

12   Q. How was work after that episode?

13   A. Tense, but I just focused on what I did

14 best. I sold computers to businesses and made them

15 feel like valued customers.

16   Q. What led to your eventual termination?

17   A. Danielle Khouri fired me based on my age.

18 The whole place was trying to be some kind of baby

19 genius factory, so they started firing older

20 workers.

21   Q. When did this change start happening?

22   A. The first shot across the bow was making

23 Danielle CEO. She was so underqualified and had no

24 experience.

25   Q. What changes did Danielle make?

Page 13

1   A. Well, we already talked about the meetings
2   about social media. That was before she even got
3   into the big chair. Then there were the putdowns,
4   the harassment. Then eventually you just noticed
5   people you came into Century with started
6   disappearing.
7   Q. Let's start with the putdowns. Can you
8   describe them.
9   A. It was subtle, but it was nonstop.
10   Danielle and her little minion, Aaron Sassower,
11   would make these snide comments toward me and some
12   older workers in meetings.
13   Q. What was the nature of these comments?
14   A. Asking us if we were following the
15   material, checking to make sure we hadn't "dozed
16   off." It was so rude and condescending.
17   Q. What did you do about any of this?
18   A. At first, I thought it was good-natured
19   ribbing, but eventually I spoke to Khouri about it
20   personally. I wasn't afraid of her.
21   Q. When did you have that conversation?
22   A. Probably June or July of YR-3.
23   Q. How did that conversation go?
24   A. I told her I was tired of the abuse and
25   tired of the comments being made by some of the

Page 14

1   newer hires. Danielle said, "Look, you know we
2   don't mean anything. The company's just going in a
3   new direction, and we hope you can keep up."
4   Q. How did you interpret that?
5   A. As a threat.
6   Q. How did the environment improve, if at
7   all, following this meeting?
8   A. It got worse, if anything. For my birthday
9   in November, they gave me this really offensive
10   card making some joke about getting old. It had a
11   cane on it or something stupid. I mean, I was 48
12   years old.
13   Q. How did you respond?
14   A. I went to Jim Stancil in HR. He and I
15   were old friends, came up through the company
16   together, and he could sympathize because he was
17   about my age.
18   Q. How did Mr. Stancil handle these
19   incidents?
20   A. He told me to keep quiet because Khouri
21   was looking for any excuse to get rid of the older
22   employees.
23   Q. How did you interpret this?
24   A. I didn't take it seriously. I was their
25   best seller, consistently outperformed other

Page 15

1   divisions. They just gave me the Employee of the
2   Decade award, for crying out loud.
3   Q. Did Mr. Stancil do anything?
4   A. No. He was clearly scared of getting
5   fired, too. He knew better than anyone, as the HR
6   Director, that they were pushing out older workers.
7   Q. How long had you worked with Mr. Stancil?
8   A. Jim had been with Century for a
9   long time. Once we switched to PC sales, we were
10   making money hand over fist, expanding rapidly, and
11   decided we needed someone to handle hiring and
12   things like that.
13   Q. What did you do when Mr. Stancil said he
14   could not help?
15   A. First, I spoke with Aaron Sassower
16   directly.
17   Q. Do you remember when this conversation
18   took place?
19   A. Yes. It was February 19, YR-2.
20   Q. What did you say?
21   A. That he had a lot to learn, and that if he
22   were smart, he'd use me and others as a resource to
23   learn how to sell rather than mock us every chance
24   he got.
25   Q. How did he respond?

Page 16

1   A. He was dismissive. He told me that
2   Danielle and others "in the brass" made it clear it
3   was time to get this company into the 21st century,
4   and that's what he was going to do.
5   Q. How did the conversation end?
6   A. I left angry and followed up with an
7   email, but he never responded to the email. But he
8   eventually came and said something about no hard
9   feelings, I don't remember. It wasn't sincere.
10   Q. How was the environment after these
11   conversations?
12   A. Worse, I would say. Now Aaron and
13   Danielle would make these jokes behind my back.
14   Q. How do you know?
15   A. Jim overheard them talking about me in the
16   board room.
17   Q. How did you respond?
18   A. I requested a transfer to Alexandria. It
19   was still in my same Nita sales territory,
20   and I just wanted out.
21   Q. When?
22   A. February YR-2.
23   Q. What was the response?
24   A. Danielle called me into her office. She
25   said the transfer wasn't going to happen, but she

SHARON WATSON vs.
CENTURY TECHNOLOGIES, INC.

Page 17

1 would try to find a position that would make me
2 happy.
3 Q. How did things go after that?
4 A. Work was better, but my sales suffered. I
5 was so stressed out about this whole environment
6 that my figures slipped, but not much.
7 Q. What ever became of the position Khouri
8 mentioned?
9 A. I knew Jeff Jordan, our CFO, planned on
10 leaving soon, and I was hoping that was the
11 position.
12 Q. Did you get the position?
13 A. No. That went to Khouri's wunderkind
14 Dakota Mackenzie. She was Vice President of Global
15 Strategies or something.
16 Q. When was the promotion?
17 A. I think it was January or February YR-2.
18 Q. How did you react?
19 A. I was furious.
20 Q. Why?
21 A. Our business was, and has always been,
22 about sales. It was about numbers. And here I
23 was, the best seller in the company's history,
24 being pushed out by someone who was really awesome
25 with Facebook.

Page 18

1 Q. Did you express this?
2 A. I did. I spoke with Danielle, and she
3 said something about "new blood" and "fresh ideas."
4 I just left and told her it was ridiculous.
5 Q. What were your sales figures like during
6 these years?
7 A. Solid. Not astronomical, but better than
8 any other division.
9 Q. When did you receive your Employee of the
10 Decade award?
11 A. Well, it was Employee of the Decade, and
12 that was in YR-4. Apparently, Century has a very
13 short memory.
14 Q. What happened when you confronted
15 Danielle?
16 A. It wasn't pretty.
17 Q. What did she say?
18 A. She told me I needed to watch myself and
19 that no one was bigger than the company.
20 Q. What was your response?
21 A. I told her I gave my life to this company,
22 and she promoted someone who'd been here five
23 minutes. It wasn't right.
24 Q. How did you leave the conversation?
25 A. Danielle said she really respected all my

Page 19

1 success selling beepers, but that there wasn't room
2 for stubborn old people at the top anymore. I
3 walked out.
4 Q. How was the environment after that
5 conversation?
6 A. Miserable. I couldn't stand being in that
7 office anymore.
8 Q. Why did you stay until your termination?
9 A. In case you haven't noticed, the job
10 marketed is soft these days, especially for someone
11 in their 50s.
12 Q. And just to clarify, you are currently
13 unemployed?
14 A. Yes. My severance helped, but I am barely
15 making ends meet now.
16
17
18
19
20
21
22
23
24
25

Page 20

1   DEPOSITION OFFICER'S CERTIFICATE
2 STATE OF NITA   )
3 COUNTY OF NITA   } ss.
)
4
5
6   I, Balinda Dunlap, hereby certify:
7   I am a duly qualified Certified Shorthand
8 Reporter in the State of Nita, holder of
9 Certificate Number CSR 10710 issued by the Court
10 Reporters Board of Nita and which is in full force
11 and effect. (Fed. R. Civ. P. 28(a)).
12   I am authorized to administer oaths or
13 affirmations pursuant to Nita Code of Civil
14 Procedure, Section 2093(b) and prior to being examined,
15 the witness was first duly sworn by me. (Fed. R. Civ.
16 P. 28(a), 30(f)(1)).
17   I am not a relative or employee or attorney or
18 counsel of any of the parties, nor am I a relative or
19 employee of such attorney or counsel, nor am I
20 financially interested in this action. (Fed. R. Civ. P.
21 28).
22   I am the deposition officer that
23 stenographically recorded the testimony in the foregoing
24 deposition and the foregoing transcript is a true record
25   / / /

A

Aaron (4)
9:20;13:10;15:15;
16:12
Absolutely (1)
4:13
abuse (1)
13:24
accountant (1)
7:2
accounting (1)
11:18
accusation (2)
12:3,7
accused (2)
11:19,22
across (1)
12:22
address (1)
2:20
addressed (1)
8:9
ads (1)
4:17
advice (1)
9:25
affected (1)
3:10
afraid (1)
13:20
again (1)
10:4
age (2)
12:17;14:17
ago (1)
9:4
Alexandria (1)
16:18
Almighty (1)
7:8
always (1)
17:21
angry (1)
16:6
anymore (4)
3:15;4:3;19:2,7
Apparently (1)
18:12
appeared (1)
2:10
appropriating (1)
11:23
area (1)
6:15
around (2)
9:24;11:5
Assistant (2)
9:8;10:25
Associates (3)
5:5;7:3;8:18
astronomical (1)

18:7
August (1)
16:22
Avenue (1)
2:22
award (2)
15:2;18:10
awesome (1)
17:24

B

baby (1)
12:18
back (6)
4:18,23;6:22;10:12;
12:5;16:13
Balinda (1)
2:7
barely (1)
19:14
Barkley (1)
2:5
Barron (1)
5:4
base (1)
7:16
based (1)
12:17
Basically (1)
6:14
became (1)
17:7
Beeper (2)
7:14,20
beepers (4)
6:15,20;10:19;19:1
behind (1)
16:13
best (5)
10:10;11:10;12:14;
14:25;17:23
better (4)
4:24;15:5;17:4;18:7
big (1)
13:3
bigger (2)
7:13;18:19
Bill (3)
11:19,22;12:4
blood (1)
18:3
blowup (1)
12:10
Board (2)
9:23;16:16
boom (1)
10:16
booming (1)
10:22
bottom (1)
7:8
bought (2)

7:13,16
bow (1)
12:22
box (1)
3:24
brand (1)
7:17
brass (1)
16:2
brought (1)
9:23
Burns (1)
7:2
business (3)
6:19;10:22;17:21
businesses (3)
6:15,17;12:14

C

CALIFORNIA (4)
2:1,6,7,9
call (1)
8:10
called (5)
2:12;3:14;5:24;6:19;
16:24
calls (1)
6:14
came (5)
8:6;12:3;13:5;14:15;
16:8
Can (9)
2:20;3:6;4:9,11,22,
25;9:6;13:7;14:3
cane (1)
14:11
card (1)
14:10
cardboard (1)
3:24
care (2)
11:19,21
career (1)
5:14
case (1)
19:9
cash (1)
11:6
cellular (1)
6:16
Century (8)
6:3,10;11:7,11;13:5;
15:8;16:3;18:12
CEO (6)
3:16,20;4:14,18;7:2;
12:23
CEO's (1)
3:14
Certified (2)
2:7,13
CFO (1)
17:9

chair (2)
11:10;13:3
chance (1)
15:23
change (4)
8:1;10:13,20;12:21
changed (2)
7:10;10:14
changes (1)
12:25
charge (1)
4:16
Chatter (1)
9:2
checking (1)
13:15
chickens (1)
9:9
children (1)
9:3
city (1)
6:20
clarify (1)
19:12
class (1)
6:9
classes (2)
5:13;6:8
Classic (1)
3:11
clear (1)
16:2
clearly (1)
15:4
client (5)
5:22;7:16;9:16;
11:24,25
climbing (1)
11:13
cold (1)
6:14
college (2)
5:12;6:4
Columbia (2)
6:6;16:19
com (1)
10:16
commencing (1)
2:4
comments (3)
13:11,13,25
Community (1)
6:6
company (18)
4:12,14;7:5,14;8:13,
24;9:1,14,22;10:4,13,
20;11:2,9;14:15;16:3;
18:19,21
company's (2)
14:2;17:23
complained (1)
8:24
computers (2)

10:21;12:14
condescending (1)
13:16
confronted (1)
18:14
connection (1)
9:15
consistently (1)
14:25
conversation (7)
4:1;13:21,23;15:17;
16:5;18:24;19:5
conversations (1)
16:11
cord! (1)
11:11
County (1)
2:8
course (2)
3:1;6:22
Court (1)
2:5
cow (1)
11:6
coworkers (1)
10:7
crazy (2)
6:18;10:8
created (1)
10:3
crying (1)
15:2
current (1)
2:23
currently (3)
2:24;3:3;19:12
customers (4)
4:17;9:5;10:11;
12:15

D

Dakota (1)
17:14
Danielle (16)
4:7,11;9:7,13,19;
12:17,23,25;13:10;
14:1;16:2,13,24;18:2,
15,25
date (2)
8:3,4
day (2)
2:4;14:9
days (2)
3:2;19:10
deal (2)
7:19;8:5
dearth (1)
14:8
Decade (3)
15:2;18:10,11
decided (1)
15:11

degree (1)
  5:11
department (1)
  5:21
describe (1)
  13:8
Development (3)
  7:21;11:24,25
different (2)
  4:3;5:20
Dinners (1)
  12:1
direction (3)
  4:3;8:7;14:3
directly (1)
  15:16
Director (2)
  11:1;15:6
disappearing (1)
  13:6
disciplined (2)
  12:7,11
discussed (1)
  9:12
dismissive (1)
  16:1
division (1)
  18:8
divisions (1)
  15:1
Dollar (1)
  7:9
dosed (1)
  13:15
dot (1)
  10:16
double-edged (1)
  3:11
down (1)
  7:15
drinks (1)
  12:1
duly (1)
  2:13
Dunlap (1)
  2:7
during (1)
  18:5
dying (1)
  7:14

E

earlier (1)
  8:14
earn (1)
  12:5
easy (1)
  3:1
email (2)
  16:7,7
employee (4)
  3:19;11:14;15:1;

18:9
employees (1)
  14:22
end (3)
  8:13;10:23;16:5
ends (1)
  19:15
English (1)
  6:8
entire (1)
  6:19
entry-level (1)
  6:11
environment (4)
  14:6;16:10;17:5;
  19:4
episode (1)
  12:12
especially (1)
  19:10
even (2)
  7:3;13:2
events (1)
  12:1
eventual (1)
  12:16
eventually (5)
  10:17;12:5;13:4,19;
  16:8
everyone (1)
  8:13
exact (1)
  7:23
exactly (2)
  9:17,24
excuse (1)
  14:21
executive (2)
  3:23;18:11
executives (1)
  7:20
expanding (1)
  15:10
expected (1)
  11:16
experience (2)
  3:12;12:24
explanation (1)
  4:5
exploded (1)
  11:6
express (1)
  18:1

F

face (1)
  9:14
factory (1)
  12:19
fall (1)
  7:25
family (1)

5:9
fax (2)
  6:15;10:18
February (2)
  15:19;17:17
feel (1)
  12:15
feelings (1)
  16:9
fell (1)
  11:9
felt (1)
  6:19
few (4)
  5:10;6:2,8;9:19
fields (1)
  3:3
figured (1)
  5:25
figures (2)
  17:6;18:5
find (1)
  17:1
finish (1)
  5:12
fired (2)
  12:17;15:5
firing (1)
  12:19
firm (4)
  5:5,20,21;8:13
first (7)
  4:25;5:7;6:10;11:8;
  12:22;13:18;15:15
fist (1)
  15:10
five (3)
  7:1;9:4;18:22
focus (1)
  9:1
focused (4)
  5:14;7:7;8:24;12:13
followed (1)
  16:6
following (2)
  13:14;14:7
follows (1)
  2:16
forget (1)
  11:8
formally (1)
  12:11
Fortune (1)
  11:8
FRANCISCO (3)
  2:1,6,9
fresh (1)
  18:3
friend (1)
  5:9
friends (2)
  9:20;14:15
fun (1)

6:9
funds (1)
  11:23
furious (1)
  17:19

G

gave (3)
  14:9;15:1;18:21
genius (1)
  12:19
giant (2)
  6:16,23
Global (1)
  17:14
good (2)
  5:14;7:15
good-natured (1)
  13:18
Google (1)
  4:17
Gosh (1)
  4:23
grew (2)
  11:6,7
guru (1)
  4:15

H

Hampton (1)
  9:20
hand (1)
  15:10
handle (2)
  14:18;15:11
hands-on (1)
  3:7
happen (2)
  11:11;16:25
happened (3)
  7:12;11:12;18:14
happening (1)
  12:21
happy (1)
  17:2
harassment (1)
  13:4
hard (1)
  16:8
heading (1)
  8:1
hear (1)
  4:4
help (1)
  15:14
helped (1)
  19:14
herein (1)
  2:12
hires (1)
  14:1

hiring (1)
  15:11
history (1)
  17:23
hope (1)
  14:3
hoping (1)
  17:10
hour (1)
  2:4
HR (3)
  3:24;14:14;15:5
Human (1)
  3:20
humored (1)
  10:1

I

idea (1)
  9:4
ideas (1)
  18:3
improve (1)
  14:6
incidents (1)
  14:19
increasing (1)
  4:16
Internet (2)
  10:9;11:6
interpret (2)
  14:4,23
interrupt (1)
  4:9
into (10)
  3:14;6:23;7:5;8:1;
  11:6,9;13:3,5;16:3,24
Ionia (1)
  2:21

J

January (1)
  17:17
Jeff (1)
  17:9
Jim (10)
  7:1,13,18,20;8:6;
  11:1,9;14:14;15:8;
  16:15
job (6)
  3:10;4:25;5:6,8,15;
  19:9
jobs (1)
  6:5
joke (1)
  14:10
jokes (1)
  16:13
Jordan (1)
  17:9
Josh (1)
  17:9

9:20
July (1)
13:22
June (1)
13:22

K

keep (3)
8:7;14:3,20
keeping (1)
12:9
kept (1)
11:13
Khouri (8)
4:7,11,13;9:7;12:17;
13:19;14:20;17:7
Khouri's (1)
17:13
kind (7)
6:17;7:14,16,19;
11:25;12:2,18
kinds (1)
10:8
knack (1)
5:23
knew (4)
8:14;10:17;15:5;
17:9

L

ladder (1)
11:13
late (2)
4:23;15:8
law (2)
5:5,20
lawyers (1)
4:8
leadership (2)
8:2;9:3
learn (3)
5:25;15:21,23
leave (2)
7:18;18:24
leaving (1)
17:10
led (3)
9:17;12:10,16
left (4)
5:10;8:10;16:6;18:4
life (2)
4:21;18:21
line (1)
7:8
literally (1)
4:15
little (2)
9:19;13:10
live (1)
2:21
long (6)

4:19;6:1;8:12;9:22,
23;15:7
longer (1)
11:16
Look (1)
14:1
looking (3)
2:25;3:3;14:21
lot (3)
3:12;8:18;15:21
loud (1)
15:2

M

ma'am (1)
2:18
machines (2)
6:16;10:18
Mackenzie (1)
17:14
mainly (2)
3:5;10:14
major (1)
3:23
making (6)
6:14;11:13;12:22;
14:10;15:10;19:15
managerial (1)
3:6
many (1)
6:25
mark (1)
11:14
marketed (1)
19:10
marketing (3)
3:5;4:15;9:8
material (1)
13:15
matters (1)
11:18
May (1)
3:14
mean (10)
3:18,19;5:16;7:6;
8:4;10:2,3;11:4;14:2,
11
media (6)
4:16;8:25;9:1,10,10;
13:2
meet (2)
3:16;19:15
meeting (1)
14:7
meetings (3)
9:18;13:1,12
memory (1)
18:13
mentioned (3)
7:5;10:4;17:8
merger (3)
7:23;8:21;10:12

mid-'90s (3)
7:11,12;11:5
minion (1)
13:10
minutes (1)
18:23
Miserable (1)
19:6
misunderstanding (2)
11:20;12:9
mock (1)
15:23
Monday (1)
2:3
money (2)
5:14;15:10
monstrosity (3)
6:23;7:6;8:10
months (2)
8:5,5
more (1)
9:6
much (2)
8:24;17:6
Murray (1)
7:2
myself (1)
18:18

N

name (1)
2:18
named (2)
4:18;11:14
names (1)
7:4
natural (1)
5:24
nature (1)
13:13
needed (5)
3:15;4:2;5:11;15:11;
18:18
new (7)
5:25;8:7;9:10,15;
14:3;16:19;18:3
newer (1)
14:1
next (3)
5:15,16,18
night (1)
5:13
nonstop (1)
13:9
noticed (2)
13:4;19:9
November (1)
14:9
numbers (1)
17:22

O

o0o- (2)
2:2,17
occupation (1)
2:23
OCTOBER (2)
2:1,4
off (1)
13:16
offensive (1)
14:9
office (3)
3:14;16:24;19:7
official (1)
8:1
old (6)
3:8;6:16;14:10,12,
15;19:2
older (6)
8:18,19;12:19;13:12;
14:21;15:6
Once (1)
15:9
One (3)
5:22;9:20;18:19
Only (1)
6:2
opened (2)
5:10;6:3
opposed (1)
3:20
others (3)
9:13;15:22;16:2
out (11)
5:5;7:13;8:5;10:8;
12:4;15:2,6;16:20;
17:5,24;19:3
outperformed (1)
14:25
over (2)
9:3;15:10
overheard (1)
16:15
overqualified (1)
3:12

P

part (3)
4:24;5:20;8:12
partners (1)
5:23
PC (1)
15:9
PCs (2)
10:22;11:5
people (10)
4:6;6:25;7:7;8:15,16,
20;10:6,18;13:5;19:2
personal (2)
10:21;11:23

personally (2)
2:9;13:20
phase (1)
8:6
phones (2)
5:7;6:16
place (3)
7:24;12:18;15:18
Plaintiff (1)
2:12
planned (2)
5:13;17:9
pm (1)
2:5
point (2)
10:13,24
position (15)
5:9,16,17,18,22;6:2,
10,11;10:24;11:2,15;
17:1,7,11,12
positions (1)
3:6
potential (1)
9:15
pottery (1)
6:9
power (1)
7:19
presence (1)
4:16
President (2)
7:21;17:14
pretty (2)
11:20;18:16
Probably (2)
7:11;13:22
problem (1)
8:22
process (1)
8:12
profile (1)
10:4
promoted (3)
11:1,12;18:22
promotion (2)
5:19;17:16
properly (1)
12:10
prospects (1)
3:10
provide (1)
4:5
pushed (1)
17:24
pushing (1)
15:6
putdowns (2)
13:3,7

Q

quickly (1)
11:20

quiet (1)
14:20

R

rapidly (1)
15:10
rather (1)
15:23
react (1)
17:18
real (1)
5:23
really (5)
4:15;5:19;14:9;
17:24;18:25
Reardon (4)
7:1,13,18;11:1
receipts (1)
12:9
receive (1)
18:9
Regional (1)
10:25
reigns (1)
7:9
relation (1)
4:12
relations (1)
5:22
remember (6)
7:3,23;9:17,24;
15:17;16:9
REMEMBERED (1)
2:3
Reporter (2)
2:8,14
Reporters (1)
2:5
representative (1)
3:21
requested (1)
16:18
resource (1)
15:22
Resources (1)
3:21
respected (1)
18:25
respond (3)
14:13;15:25;16:17
responded (1)
16:7
response (2)
16:23;18:20
responsibilities (1)
6:13
ribbing (1)
13:19
rid (1)
14:21
ridiculous (1)
18:4

right (3)
8:20;10:16;18:23
Rockpoint (2)
5:5;6:6
room (3)
4:6;16:16;19:1
rude (1)
13:16

S

sale (1)
11:8
Sales (11)
3:5;7:3;8:18,25;
10:10;11:1;15:9;16:19;
17:4,22;18:5
salespeople (1)
6:21
same (1)
16:19
SAN (3)
2:1,6,8
Sassower (3)
9:20;13:10;15:15
Sauganash (1)
2:21
saved (1)
11:2
saw (2)
7:15;8:22
scared (1)
15:4
second (1)
5:1
secretary (1)
5:7
sell (2)
6:20;15:23
seller (2)
14:25;17:23
selling (5)
5:24;6:15;10:14,21;
19:1
semesters (1)
5:10
send (1)
3:23
seriously (1)
14:24
services (1)
4:2
sessions (1)
9:11
severance (1)
19:14
Shar (1)
11:10
sharing (1)
7:19
SHARON (2)
2:11,19
short (1)

18:13
Shorthand (2)
2:8,14
shot (1)
12:22
sincere (1)
16:9
slipped (1)
17:6
slowing (1)
7:15
small (2)
6:22;11:18
smart (1)
15:22
snide (1)
13:11
social (5)
4:16;8:25;9:1,10;
13:2
soft (1)
19:10
software (1)
10:22
sold (1)
12:14
Solid (1)
18:7
someone (4)
15:11;17:24;18:22;
19:10
sometime (1)
7:25
soon (1)
17:10
sorry (3)
4:9,10,13
sounds (1)
6:18
speaking (1)
8:16
specific (2)
4:22;9:6
spirits (1)
8:8
spoke (3)
13:19;15:15;18:2
sporting (1)
12:1
spring (1)
9:9
Stancil (5)
14:14,18;15:3,7,13
stand (1)
19:6
standard (1)
6:11
start (4)
5:17;8:2;12:21;13:7
started (5)
5:4;7:7;8:14;12:19;
13:5
State (1)

2:9
stay (2)
11:15;19:8
stayed (1)
7:20
still (3)
8:9;10:18;16:19
stonewalled (1)
4:7
stop (1)
10:9
Strategies (1)
17:15
strategy (1)
11:3
Street (1)
2:6
stressed (1)
17:5
stubborn (1)
19:2
study (1)
6:7
stuff (1)
10:8
stupid (1)
14:11
subordinates (1)
10:7
substance (1)
3:25
subtle (1)
13:9
success (1)
19:1
suffered (1)
17:4
Suite (1)
2:6
supposed (1)
11:24
supreme (1)
7:9
Sure (3)
5:1;9:7;13:15
switched (2)
10:21;15:9
sword (1)
3:11
sworn (1)
2:13
sympathize (1)
14:16

T

talent (1)
5:24
talked (1)
13:1
talking (1)
16:15
targeting (1)

4:17
Technologies (1)
6:3
telephone (1)
11:11
Tense (1)
12:13
terminated (3)
3:13,17,20
termination (2)
12:16;19:8
territory (1)
16:19
testified (1)
2:15
thanks (1)
11:7
thereof (1)
2:5
thought (1)
13:18
threat (1)
14:5
threw (1)
10:8
times (1)
9:14
tired (3)
8:14;13:24,25
title (2)
5:6;7:21
today (1)
6:24
together (1)
14:16
told (14)
3:15;4:2,8;5:9,23;
10:9;11:2,9;13:24;
14:20;16:1;18:4,18,21
Tons (1)
3:11
took (5)
6:9;7:24;8:4;9:3;
15:18
top (2)
12:5;19:2
toward (1)
13:11
training (1)
9:10
transfer (3)
5:20;16:18,25
transition (1)
8:6
treated (1)
8:15
trend (1)
11:7
truth (3)
2:14,15,15
try (1)
17:1
trying (2)

6:20;12:18
turned (3)
  3:9;6:23;7:5
two (1)
  7:2

U

underqualified (1)
  12:23
unemployed (3)
  2:24;4:20;19:13
up (6)
  5:10;6:3;8:8;14:3,
  15;16:6
use (2)
  11:23;15:22
using (1)
  10:18
usual (2)
  3:19;4:4

V

valued (1)
  12:15
Vice (2)
  7:21;17:14
VP (1)
  9:8

W

walked (1)
  19:3
watch (1)
  18:18
WATSON (2)
  2:11,19
way (3)
  8:14;10:17;12:5
web-based (1)
  8:25
weren't (3)
  3:23;4:2;8:19
what's (1)
  10:10
who'd (1)
  18:22
whole (3)
  2:14;12:18;17:5
winter (1)
  8:1
witness (1)
  2:12
work (7)
  2:25;3:4;5:11;8:5;
  9:4;12:12;17:4
worked (2)
  12:4;15:7
workers (3)
  12:20;13:12;15:6
working (2)

4:19;5:4
World (2)
  7:15,20
worse (2)
  14:8;16:12
wrongfully (1)
  11:22
wunderkind (1)
  17:13

X

X-14 (1)
  11:14
X-16 (1)
  10:25
X-19 (1)
  8:2
X-2 (3)
  15:19;16:22;17:17
X-3 (1)
  13:22
X-4 (1)
  18:12
X-7 (1)
  9:24
X-8 (1)
  9:24

Y

year (2)
  7:23;11:14
years (5)
  4:24;6:2;9:4;14:12;
  18:6
Yourworld (3)
  9:2,15;17:25

1

1000 (1)
  11:9
12:30 (1)
  2:5
19 (2)
  3:15;15:19
1980s (1)
  4:24
1990s (1)
  15:9

2

2001 (1)
  3:15
2003 (1)
  4:18
201 (1)
  2:5
2013 (2)
  2:1,4
2020 (1)

8:1
2025 (1)
  6:12
21st (1)
  16:3

3

30 (1)
  4:24
30s (1)
  8:19
375 (1)
  2:6

4

48 (1)
  14:11

5

50 (1)
  3:9
50s (1)
  19:11

6

6232 (1)
  2:21

7

7 (1)
  2:1
7th (1)
  2:3

EXPERT WITNESS MATERAILS (OPTIONAL)

AFFIDAVIT OF ERIN HAMMEL

I, Erin Hammel, depose and state the following, and if sworn as a witness at trial could competently testify to the following:

1. I am over the age of eighteen years and qualified to make this affidavit. I am a resident of the State of Nita and make this affidavit based on my review of the documents and other records provided to me by the parties. I have no direct or indirect interest in the outcome of this case for which I am offering observations, analysis, opinions, and testimony.

2. I am experienced in human resources (HR) administration, with over twenty years' experience in the HR field as an administrator, director of benefits, and independent consultant.

3. I received my Master's in Business Administration (MBA) from Nita Online University in May YR-10. I focused my studies on benefits administration, including administration of plans subject to the Employee Retirement Income Security Act (ERISA), defined contribution plans, and executive compensation agreements. I was a teachers' assistant with Professor David Drake for several classes on collective bargaining agreements and labor-management relations.

4. I have a certificate as a Senior Professional Expert in the American Disabilities Act from the Society for Human Resource Management, the world's largest HR professionals' society, representing 285,000 members in more than 165 countries.

5. For the past ten years, I have been providing HR consulting services to some of the largest corporations in North America on a wide variety of topics, including compliance with the Age Discrimination and Employment Act (ADEA) and related state statutes. I have revised countless Employee Handbooks and Codes of Conduct with an eye toward compliance with antidiscrimination statutes and case law.

In preparing my testimony, I reviewed the following documents:

    a. The complaint filed by the plaintiff

    b. Exhibit 1, emails exchanged between Century Technologies employees

    c. Exhibit 3, the mediation reports drafted by Jim Stancil regarding other employee disputes

    d. Exhibit 11, the "Social Media and 21st Century Sale" training deck administered by Century Technologies

    e. Exhibit 14, the Century Technologies Human Resources Manual

RECENT TRENDS IN AGE DISCRIMINATION
THROUGHOUT THE WORKFORCE

7. I have spent the past several decades working in the field of human resources and have personally witnessed clients and companies struggle with the shifting dynamic between aging employees and younger subordinates.

8. As a result of changing technology and younger employees with different priorities, older workers very often feel victimized and singled out. As an HR Consultant, I do my best to ensure that employers have the tools and resources to mitigate the disruption caused by technology and to avoid litigation risks.

9. Age discrimination complaints have dramatically increased over the past twenty years. For example, from YR-18 to YR-8, there were between 16,000 and 19,000 annual age discrimination complaints filed with the Equal Employment Opportunity Commission. Since YR-7, that number has increased to between 23,000 and 25,000 age discrimination complaints annually. While most of these suits are unsuccessful, employers are aware of this increase and have worked on their mitigation and risk management strategies.

10. One reason I have found age discrimination cases likely increase is because after the Great Recession of YR-7, older employees who were let go had a difficult time finding new employment. The average duration of unemployment for those over the age of fifty-five is nearly one year, while younger workers only have to deal with being jobless for about seven months on average.

11. Statistics also demonstrate that age discrimination seems to be worse for women when it comes to hiring. According to the National Bureau of Economic Research, résumés of older women get fewer callbacks than those of both older men and younger job applicants of either sex.

12. Age discrimination may be much more prevalent than these statistics imply. According to an AARP study, 64 percent of workers age fifty-five or older say they have experienced age discrimination at work. Similar studies also show that many people who "voluntarily" retire feel they are pushed out of their positions by their employers.

CENTURY TECHNOLOGIES'
POLICIES AND PROCEDURES

13. I have reviewed the evidence provided based on my experience in the field of human resources and passed on my experience consulting and counseling corporations on similar matters.

14. It is my opinion that Century Technologies' policies and practices were insufficient, generally, to ensure a welcoming and non-discriminatory workplace for older employees.

15. Century Technologies' Human Resources Handbook is sufficient in its anti-discrimination and anti-retaliation policies.

16. The Handbook sufficiently advises employees that Century has a policy against harassment or discrimination based on several protected categories, including discrimination based on age.

17. Additionally, the Handbook uses unique language that, if read by an employee, would imply that these provisions were drafted by Century itself—not simply copied and pasted from another document.

18. The Handbook also provides a form to submit for acts of discrimination. I often counsel employers to provide an employee a standard form on which to submit a complaint. Very often, those clients decline the invitation and instead put the onus on the employee to separately draft a complaint. Century's decision to create a standard form is a common HR best practice for encouraging open and honest reporting of discrimination.

19. A major deficiency in the policy is the mandatory mediation at the discretion of the Director of HR. Despite clear warnings that employees will not be subject to retaliation, an employee who feels that he or she may be forced to be in the same room with their harasser, or the person discriminating against them, has a deterrent effect. I counsel my clients to make mediation purely optional at the discretion of the accuser.

20. Based on the mediation reports I read, Mr. Stancil did not conduct proper mediations in a way that would lead to positive resolutions of discrimination, harassment, or misconduct allegations. As best I can tell, Mr. Stancil put the employees with disagreements in a room and forced them to talk to one other.

21. I counsel clients to bring in trained, non-biased mediators through third-party vendors. I often perform these services myself, as it removes the potential for a known colleague to be forced to mediate a crisis.

22. The social media training document was entirely inappropriate and I would have counseled any of my clients to revise it substantially.

23. As part of my responsibilities as an HR consultant, I often perform sensitivity training sessions for employees. Topics on which I have trained cover a wide range, including sexual harassment and racial discrimination.

24. I see several critical problems with the social media training document. The presentation contains several uses of coded language and images. Dinosaurs and older people using outdated technologies send a clear signal to employees over the age of forty: they are not valued, and they may be the subject of ridicule.

25. In my experience, older employees are especially sensitive to the perception they are unable to use changing technology. For example, the heavy manufacturing clients I have counseled often struggle with their employees operating new machinery. Accordingly, I counsel clients to avoid any images or words that could be insensitive.

26. Many clients often try to inject humor into a presentation. However, if is always my recommendation not to make jokes—even lighthearted ones—at the expense of any particular group. This is both a strategy for managing talent appropriately, but also a loss mitigation/litigation avoidance strategy.

27. Based on my review of the email communications between the plaintiff and representatives of Century Technologies, all parties were engaging in age-coded language. The plaintiff referred to her younger coworkers as "kids," while younger employees sarcastically referenced older employees who are "experienced."

28. Competent HR professionals are trained to be aware of the tensions within their own office. It is clear from the internal communications that these squabbles and personal disputes were open and should have been addressed more forcefully.

29. The social media training—already a topic that older employees would be anxious about, as most older employees are simply unfamiliar with rapidly evolving computer technologies—would have been highly distressful to older employees.

30. I would have counseled my clients to remove the coded language contained in the PowerPoint slide show, including the image of the dinosaur. A training on a sensitive topics like improving the use of social media should be generally applicable and not blatantly targeted toward any one particular group.

31. I conclude, for the reasons stated herein, that Century Technologies' policies, procedures for reporting harassment and discrimination, and conduct of trainings are not consistent with best practices commonly advocated by HR professionals.

FURTHER AFFIANT SAYETH NAUGHT.

Erin Hammel

Erin Hammel

CERTIFICATION

Under the penalties as provided by law pursuant to Section 1-109 of the Code of Civil Procedure, the undersigned certifies that the statements set forth in this instrument are true and correct.

Erin Hammel

Erin Hammel

ERIN HAMMEL

100 E. 14TH STREET
NITA CITY, NITA 98144
hrconsult@peopleperson.nita

PROFILE

Dedicated human resources professional with 20+ years of experience. Manages all matters of payroll, benefits compliance, tax and accounting compliance, leave and disability troubleshooting, sexual harassment training, and all other HR matters. I have been managing a private HR Consulting Firm for the past ten years with incredible success for each of my clients.

PROFESSIONAL EXPERIENCE

People Person, LLC   **11/1/YR-10 – Present**
Founder and Managing Partner   **Nita City, Nita**

- Provide benefits, payroll, and labor management services to Fortune 500 Companies across the world including John Deere, UPS, ABF Freight, and several others
- Conduct trainings for clients on harassment prevention, including sexual harassment, racial discrimination, and sexual orientation sensitivity training
- Draft and revise 100+ Employee Handbooks and Codes of Conduct for clients in Nita and across the U.S.

Nita City Colleges   **6/1/YR-13 – 10/1/YR-10**
Assistant Director, Benefits Department   **Nita City, Nita**

- Administered medical and dental insurance plans, 401(k) and deferred compensation plans, medical and FMLA leave, and ERISA matters for faculty of 100+ professors, administrators, and other employees
- Delivered training presentations explaining benefits and changes to benefit plans

Nita Hotels Worldwide, Inc. – Nita City Inn   **8/1/YR-16 – 5/1/YR-13**
Assistant Payroll Supervisor   **Nita City, Nita**

- Oversaw installation and maintenance of fracking equipment for safety compliance
- Drafted procedural documents to ensure consistent operations

EDUCATION, CERTIFICATES, & ASSOCIATIONS

Society for Human Resource Management (SHRM) Certificate – Senior Professional Expert in Americans with Disabilities Act (ADA)

Associations and Memberships
  - Society for Human Resource Management, Vice Chair ADA Committee
  - International Personnel Assessment Council
  - Personnel Testing Council of Southern Nita

Nita Online University (Nita)
Master's of Business Administration, May YR-10

University of Wisconsin (Madison, WI)
B.A., English, May YR-18

JUROR FOCUS GROUP

This case file features a 100-minute recording of a focus group of jurors who listened to the testimony of witnesses and examined the exhibits, then discussed their impressions of both.

Please do not view the recording until your instructor directs you to do so. At his or her discretion, your instructor will either screen it in class or request you watch it outside of class, so please await instruction.

When directed, you may access the recording here:

http://bit.ly/2K3xrRv

Passcode: Wat17FocusGp

Please note the passcode is case sensitive.

APPENDICES

Appendix A

LOCAL RULES FOR MOCK TRIALS AND PRETRIAL CONFERENCES

MOCK TRIAL

1. Trial Realism

The trial should be conducted as realistically as possible.

Each participant—judge, lawyer, witness—should stay in "role." E.g., don't stop the trial for critique; no objections on the ground that it's not in the script; if you get mixed up or lose your place, stay in character as if you were in front of a real jury; regroup and continue.

2. Trial Materials

The factual basis for the trial is the case file, which is available to all persons participating in the trial.

If a witness testifies inconsistent with the materials in the case file, the witness may be impeached. For the purpose of impeachment at trial, it is assumed that the statement or deposition was given, read, and signed by the witness.

The objection that "it's not in the script or case file" will not be permitted.

3. Pretrial Order

A pretrial order summarizing the results of the pretrial conference shall be given to the trial judge the morning of the trial. The pretrial order shall be signed by counsel for both sides and cover the following:

a) Issues to be determined at trial

b) Admissions and stipulations

c) Witness list

d) Exhibit list

e) Stipulations regarding exhibits

f) Motions in limine

g) Proposed jury instructions

h) Any further matters

4. Motions

Procedural motions at trial are discouraged. If a party wishes to make a motion in limine relating to the evidence, it should be raised and heard at the pretrial conference. No more than two motions per party are permitted.

5. Documents, Charts, Exhibits

All documents, charts, and exhibits of any kind that will be used at trial must be marked for identification. Plaintiffs use 1, 2, 3, etc. Defendants use A, B, C, etc. This should be done before the pretrial conference.

A document should not be marked for identification by both parties. If both parties wish to use a particular document, it should be marked as one party's exhibit and then it is available for use at trial by any party.

6. Stipulations

All stipulations should be reached between counsel before the pretrial conference if at all possible. Any stipulations reached after the pretrial conference should be put in writing, signed by counsel for both parties, and appended to the pretrial order.

7. Time Limits

Opening statement—10 minutes per side maximum

Plaintiff case-in-chief (including cross-examination)—75 minutes

Defendant case-in-chief (including cross-examination)—75 minutes

Closing argument—20 minutes per side; plaintiff can reserve 5 minutes for rebuttal

It is important that the trial proceed within the time guidelines so that time is available for critique.

8. Jury Selection

The jury will be seated prior to the start of trial. No voir dire will take place.

Counsel might note those jurors whom they may have challenged and then after the verdict compare their evaluation with the juror's actual vote.

9. Counsels' Division of Responsibility

Counsel may divide the opening statements, summations, and witness examinations in any way they wish. However, it shall be an even division of labor. Only one counsel per witness examination is permitted. See Rule 12, below.

10. Objections

Objections and motions should be made and determined realistically. Sidebar conferences should be kept to a minimum.

No objections may be made that "those facts are not within the materials." If you believe that the witness has gone outside the trial materials, then impeach the witness on cross-examination by using his or her statement or deposition.

11. Adverse Witnesses

Adverse witnesses may be called. However, each party may call only one adverse witness and is subject to time limits of ten minutes for adverse examination and five minutes for cross-examination. The cross-examination is limited to the scope of the adverse examination. Any matters covered during the adverse examination may not be covered again during the case-in-chief unless within the court's discretion and the interests of justice so require.

12. One Counsel to a Witness

Only one lawyer may make objections or participate in the examination of any given witness. The trial partner may not ask questions or make objections during that examination, but should always be unobtrusively aiding her partner as part and parcel of a team.

13. No Exclusion of Witnesses

A motion to exclude witnesses may be made as a matter of form for the experience of doing it. Such motion can be made orally and must be made before examination of witnesses commences. However, witnesses shall not be excluded at the trial.

14. Jury Instructions

Proposed jury instructions are limited to those provided in this case file. No additional instructions will be permitted unless authorized by the pretrial judge.

15. Critique

When the jury retires to deliberate, the judge will critique counsel's performance.

16. Comments by the Jury

After the verdict is returned, the jury should be invited to comment on the case and counsel's performance. The judge should poll the jury. Thereafter, the judge will thank and excuse the jury. Each juror will then have the opportunity to express their comments.

Counsel is permitted to talk with the jury regarding the deliberations and counsel's performance during the trial. This is an excellent opportunity for a learning experience. Counsel should utilize it to discover the jury's perceptions of the case and counsel's performance, not to quibble with the jury regarding the verdict. The verdict itself—who won or lost—is not important as it is a simulated trial; what is important in the learning process is how the jury perceived the case. What the jury thought was significant is the key element for discussion.

Counsel cannot impeach the jury verdict or win this case on appeal, but they can learn why the jury did what it did. Counsel should use the time well, as it will pay many dividends.

17. Evidence

The students have learned the Federal Rules of Evidence (FRE). Many of the visiting judges preside using their own state evidence code. For that reason, please state the objection itself, not just the rule number. Have available the FRE and the state evidence code section. E.g., "Your Honor, I object on the ground that the question is leading, FRE 611(c), EC 767(a)," as opposed to, "I object under FRE 611(c)."

PRETRIAL CONFERENCE

A pretrial conference (PTC) will be held with your instructor or trial judge in the week or days before each trial. The following is an agenda for the PTC. The indicated items must be prepared before the conference to ensure that it proceeds smoothly and within the time schedule. Counsel shall prepare a joint proposed pretrial order and include these items for each side.

1. Meet and Confer

All counsel are to meet and confer prior to the PTC. This should occur no later than one day prior to the PTC. Counsel shall exchange any necessary papers and serve the papers on the presiding PTC judge (email service is acceptable). Any agreements or stipulations should be worked out at this time.

2. Issues

The issues to be resolved at trial should be listed. A short statement of one's client's claim(s) or defense(s) should be included.

3. Admissions in the Pleadings

Any admissions in the pleadings should be set forth with a citation to the paragraph and page number. Any disputes as to whether an admission has been made should be raised and resolved at the PTC.

4. Stipulations

Any stipulations of facts or other stipulations relating to any aspect of the case (except exhibits) should be raised at this point in the PTC.

Any stipulations not resolved in the "meet and confer" session should be brought to the attention of the judge for possible action by the court.

5. Witness List

Each side shall prepare a list of their witnesses in the order they will be called at trial. Only the witnesses listed in the trial materials will be permitted.

6. List of Exhibits

Each side shall prepare before the PTC a list of all documents, charts, and exhibits of any kind that will be *used at the trial*. All exhibits must be marked for identification: plaintiffs use 1, 2, 3, etc., and defendants use A, B, C, etc.

The list of exhibits and marking for identification should include any documents used for impeachment, as the record should reflect any documents used during the trial even though it is not introduced or received in evidence.

An example and suggested format for the list of exhibits follows:

Plaintiff's List of Exhibits

No.	Title	Stipulation
1	Life Insurance Policy	Authentic
2	Letter from John Smith to Assure Insurance	
3	Deposition of William Jones	Authentic
4	Statement by Robert Hall	Authentic

7. Stipulations Regarding Exhibits

There are two basic stipulations pertaining to exhibits: admissibility and authenticity.

A stipulation to the admissibility of an exhibit means that it will automatically be received into evidence when it is offered at trial. Note that the exhibit must be formally offered, on the record, at the trial unless the judge at the PTC has specifically ordered that it be received in evidence at that time. Note that it is often best not to stipulate so that counsel may ask questions of the witness in front of the jury regarding the foundation.

A stipulation to the authenticity of an exhibit means that the document is authentic. At trial, counsel must lay the necessary foundation for its admissibility.

8.   Motions

All motions shall be written motions. The motion shall include a statement of the motion itself, relevant facts, points and authorities, argument, prayer for relief, and a conclusion. All parties shall have been served with the motion at least two days prior to the PTC. Lengthy research is not expected.

Procedural motions are discouraged.

Motions in limine

Motions to limit or exclude evidence at the trial should be made at this point in the PTC. Motions in limine are usually made for evidence that is clearly inadmissible or for evidence that is of such a nature that once the jury has heard it the cautionary or limiting instruction will not be effective (often characterized as "you cannot unring a bell").

The judge at the PTC will either rule on the motion at that time or reserve the matter to be handled at trial.

- The judge will rule on the motion at the PTC when the evidence is such that even at this preliminary stage of the proceeding the law is clear that it is either inadmissible or admissible.

- The judge will reserve ruling until trial when the admissibility of the evidence depends on how the facts are developed at trial. That is, a foundation for its admissibility must be laid at trial, the relevance of the evidence may or may not outweigh the prejudicial impact depending on what facts are developed at trial, or the judge determines that the evidentiary point is such that it is best determined within the context of the facts as they are developed at trial.

If the judge grants the motion in limine, the evidence, of course, may not be mentioned in the opening statements or otherwise brought to the attention of the jury by the counsel who opposed the motion. Many lawyers do not consider this sufficient protection since a witness may "inadvertently" blurt out the evidence at trial. The revealing of the evidence completely circumvents the motion in limine and forces the lawyer to choose between requesting a mistrial and gambling on the jury verdict, a poor choice under any circumstance. To prevent this, many lawyers who are successful on a motion in limine then request the court to order opposing counsel to instruct their witnesses not to mention or allude to the evidence. Most judges will also add that they are holding counsel responsible for the conduct of their witnesses in this regard.

If the judge reserves the motion in limine for trial, attention should be given to the use of the evidence in the opening statements. The proponent of the evidence should consider that mentioning the evidence in the opening statement may be sufficient grounds for a mistrial if the evidence is later ruled inadmissible. However, the enticement to get the evidence out early and up front in the minds of the jury is often so great that opposing counsel will gamble that it is admissible or not sufficiently inflammatory for a mistrial.

Therefore, when a motion is reserved, counsel should make a motion requesting that the evidence not be mentioned in the opening statement or otherwise brought to the attention of the jury until the court has had an opportunity to rule on the admissibility of the evidence. It is an eminently fair request and is usually granted. If this request is granted, as in the prior situation, counsel should request the court to order opposing counsel to instruct their witnesses not to mention the evidence. Counsel should instruct the witness that she is not permitted to testify about that evidence unless she is specifically asked about it.

If a motion in limine has been reserved for trial and counsel has been instructed not to bring the evidence to the attention of the jury until the court has ruled, the proper procedure is for counsel at the appropriate time during the trial (the foundation has been laid or the facts are fully developed) to approach the bench and request a ruling on the admissibility of the evidence that was the subject of the motion in limine.

The rulings of the judge at the PTC shall *not* be relitigated with the trial judge the morning of trial. The trial judge should be aware of the action taken on the motions in limine from the written pretrial order. Counsel may wish to direct the trial judge's attention to the pretrial order for informational purposes, particularly any motions that were reserved for action during the trial.

9. Pretrial Order

Counsel should have a joint proposed pretrial order prepared at the time of the PTC, which includes all of the above items.

Any motions in limine can be listed by title with a space for the court's ruling, and the actual motion presented in a separate document. If the order is accurately phrased, the court strikes "proposed" and signs the order. Otherwise, an order will have to be prepared, approved as accurate by opposing counsel, and later presented to the court for signature. All counsel must sign the court's signed order prior to the trial starting. The trial judge must be given a copy of the final order signed by the court and all counsel.

10. Jury Instructions

Jury instructions have been provided in the trial materials. Preliminary and general jury instructions are included. Specific jury instructions relating to the law and facts of the particular case are with the trial materials for that case.

No additional jury instructions will be permitted unless specifically authorized by the judge at the PTC.

Proposed jury instructions should be presented to the court with the final pretrial order. Objections to any instruction should be brought up at the PTC. All of the instructions will be settled at that time. (Normally, the court finalizes the instructions before closing argument.) At the end of the trial, the court reads the instructions to the jury. Counsel should have their own copy to review at the same time to ensure the instructions were read properly, and to object if read improperly. Otherwise, counsel may lose the issue for appeal. The judge and the instructor each need a copy of the instructions at the time of the trial.

11. Trial Binders

One trial binder per team is due at the end of the trial and will be returned at the last class. The trial binders shall reflect and contain all items necessary for trial, including the team's organization and preparation.

12.   Other Matters

Any matters relating to the simulated nature of the trial or the trial materials should be raised at this point. If counsel have a problem or foresee any difficulties relating to the simulated nature of the trial, it should be discussed at the PTC so that the trial runs smoothly and in a realistic fashion.

Remember, this is your show. It is up to you to make sure that everyone is informed of everything you feel they need to know. It is also up to you to make sure that counsel, the court, and the instructor have all necessary copies. Good luck, and have fun.

Appendix B

STATE OF NITA
COMPILED STATUTES

(775 NCS § 5/1-101)

Sec. 1-101. Short Title. This Act shall be known and may be cited as the Nita Civil Rights Act.

(775 NCS § 5/1-102)

Sec. 1-102. Declaration of Policy. It is the public policy of this State:

(A)   Freedom from Unlawful Discrimination. To secure for all individuals within Nita the freedom from discrimination against any individual because of his or her race, color, religion, sex, national origin, ancestry, age, order of protection status, marital status, physical or mental disability, military status, sexual orientation, or unfavorable discharge from military service in connection with employment, real estate transactions, access to financial credit, and the availability of public accommodations.

REDACTED

(775 NCS § 5/1-103)

Sec. 1-103. General Definitions. When used in this Act, unless the context requires otherwise, the term:

(A)   Age. "Age" means the chronological age of a person who is at least forty years old, except with regard to any practice described in Section 2-102, insofar as that practice concerns training or apprenticeship programs. In the case of training or apprenticeship programs, for the purposes of Section 2-102, "age" means the chronological age of a person who is eighteen but not yet forty years old. Condition of birth or functional disorder and which characteristic:

REDACTED

(Q)   Unlawful Discrimination. "Unlawful discrimination" means discrimination against a person because of his or her race, color, religion, national origin, ancestry, age, sex, marital status, order of protection status, disability, military status, sexual orientation, or unfavorable discharge from military service as those terms are defined in this Section.

ARTICLE 2. EMPLOYMENT

(775 NCS § 5/2-101)

Sec. 2-101. Definitions. The following definitions are applicable strictly in the context of this Article.

(A)   Employee.

    (1)   "Employee" includes:

        (a)   Any individual performing services for remuneration within this State for an employer;

        (b)   An apprentice;

        (c)   An applicant for any apprenticeship.

    (2)   "Employee" does not include:

        (a)   Domestic servants in private homes;

        (b)   Individuals employed by persons who are not "employers" as defined by this Act;

        (c)   Elected public officials or the members of their immediate personal staffs;

        (d)   Principal administrative officers of the State or of any political subdivision, municipal corporation, or other governmental unit or agency;

        (e)   A person in a vocational rehabilitation facility certified under federal law who has been designated an evaluee, trainee, or work activity client.

(B)   Employer.

    (1)   "Employer" includes:

        (a)   Any person employing fifteen or more employees within Nita during twenty or more calendar weeks within the calendar year of or preceding the alleged violation;

(b)   Any person employing one or more employees when a complainant alleges civil rights violation due to unlawful discrimination based upon his or her physical or mental disability unrelated to ability or sexual harassment;

(c)   The State and any political subdivision, municipal corporation, or other governmental unit or agency, without regard to the number of employees;

(d)   Any party to a public contract without regard to the number of employees;

(e)   A joint apprenticeship or training committee without regard to the number of employees.

(2)   "Employer" does not include any religious corporation, association, educational institution, society, or non-profit nursing institution conducted by and for those who rely upon treatment by prayer through spiritual means in accordance with the tenets of a recognized church or religious denomination with respect to the employment of individuals of a particular religion to perform work connected with the carrying on by such corporation, association, educational institution, society or non-profit nursing institution of its activities.

****REDACTED***

(775 NCS § 5/2-102)

Sec. 2-102. Civil Rights Violations-Employment. It is a civil rights violation:

(A)   Employers. For any employer to refuse to hire, to segregate, or to act with respect to recruitment, hiring, promotion, renewal of employment, selection for training or apprenticeship, discharge, discipline, tenure or terms, privileges or conditions of employment on the basis of unlawful discrimination or citizenship status.

REDACTED

ARTICLE 6. ADDITIONAL CIVIL RIGHTS VIOLATIONS

(775 NCS § 5/6-101)

Sec. 6-101. Additional Civil Rights Violations. It is a civil rights violation for a person, or for two or more persons to conspire to:

(A)   Retaliation. Retaliate against a person because he or she has opposed that which he or she reasonably and in good faith believes to be unlawful discrimination, sexual harassment in employment, or sexual harassment in elementary, secondary, and higher education, discrimination based on citizenship status in employment, or because he or she has made a charge, filed a complaint, testified, assisted, or participated in an investigation, proceeding, or hearing under this Act;

(B)   Aiding and Abetting; Coercion. Aid, abet, compel or coerce a person to commit any violation of this Act;

(C)   Interference. Willfully interfere with the performance of a duty or the exercise of a power by the commission or one of its members or representatives of the department or one of its officers or employees.

(D)   Definitions. For the purposes of this Section, "sexual harassment" and "citizenship status" shall have the meaning as defined in Section 2-101 of this Act.

JURY INSTRUCTIONS

Preliminary Instructions Given Prior to the Evidence

1. You have been selected as jurors and have taken an oath to well and truly try this cause. This trial will last one day.

2. During the progress of the trial, there will be periods of time when the Court recesses. During those periods of time, you must not talk about this case among yourselves or with anyone else. The attorneys are not allowed to speak with you, so do not attempt to do so.

3. You should keep an open mind. You should not form or express an opinion during the trial and should reach no conclusion in this case until you have heard all of the evidence, the arguments of the counsel, and the final instructions as to the law that will be given to you by the Court.

4. First, the attorneys will have an opportunity to make opening statements. These statements are not evidence and should be considered only as a preview of what the attorneys expect the evidence will be. Following opening statements, witnesses will be called to testify. They will be placed under oath and questioned.

5. It is counsel's right and duty to object where testimony or other evidence is being offered that he or she believes is not admissible. When the Court sustains an objection, the jurors must disregard the question, draw no inference nor speculation as to what the answer would have been if the witness were allowed to answer. When the Court overrules an objection, the jurors must not give that evidence any different weight than if the objection had not been made.

6. At the conclusion of evidence of both sides, the attorneys will give closing arguments. Closing arguments are made by the attorneys to discuss the facts and circumstances in the case and should be confined to the evidence and to reasonable inferences to be drawn therefrom. Finally, just before you retire to consider your verdict, I will give you further instructions on the law that applies to this case.

Final Jury Instructions—Applicable Law

1. The Court will now instruct you on the law governing this case. You must arrive at a verdict by unanimous vote, applying the law, as you are now instructed, to the facts as you have observed and find them to be.

2. The plaintiff, Sharon Watson, has filed a claim against the defendant, Century Technologies, Inc. for age discrimination. The defendant denies the claim.

3. The defendant, a corporation, can only act through its employees, and the relevant employees are the ones who made the adverse employment decision of which the plaintiff complains herein.

4. Under the Nita Civil Rights Act (NCRA), it is unlawful for any employer to intentionally discriminate against an individual who is forty years of age or older because of his or her age.

5. The NCRA makes it unlawful to terminate a person's employment on the basis of age.

6. To prove her claim of a violation of the NCRA, the plaintiff must establish each of the three elements of her claim by a preponderance of the evidence.

7. The three essential elements of the plaintiff's claim are:

    a. That the defendant took an adverse employment action against the plaintiff, specifically, terminating her employment;

    b. That at the time the adverse action was taken, the plaintiff was at least forty years old; and

    c. That the plaintiff's age was a determining factor in the defendant's decision to take adverse action.

8. To establish a claim of age discrimination, the plaintiff must prove by preponderance of the evidence that her age was a "determining factor" in the defendant's decision. Age was a "determining factor" if it made a difference in the defendant's decision.

Damages

[NB: If damages are to be determined in another proceeding, read the following instruction number 11. Otherwise, continue with the below Compensatory and Liquidated Damage Instructions.]

11. You need not concern yourself with damages at this time.

OR

12. Damages—Compensatory Damages

Under the NCRA, a successful plaintiff is entitled to recover lost wages and benefits, including wage increases. The amount of wages and benefits due is determined by calculating the amount that would have been earned from the date of adverse action to the date you, the jury, return a verdict, unless the plaintiff would have been terminated or discharged for non-discriminatory reasons prior to trial. In the latter circumstances, lost wages and benefits are calculated form the date of the adverse action to the date such discharge would have occurred.

13. Damages—Liquidated Damages

   If you find that the defendant's violation of the NCRA was "willful," you must award the plaintiff liquidated damages—that is, an additional amount equal to the lost wages and benefits you award. Liquidated damages must be awarded to the plaintiff in addition to the lost wages and benefits she receives.

14. The defendant acted willfully if it deliberately, intentionally, and knowingly took adverse action against the plaintiff because of her age and the defendant knew that such conduct was unlawful or showed reckless disregard of whether such conduct was unlawful or not—that is, the defendant knew there was a high probability that such conduct was unlawful but went ahead anyway.

Concluding Instruction

   Ladies and gentleman of the jury, this is the conclusion of the instructions, and it is now time to retire to the jury room, where you will choose a foreperson and begin your deliberations.

   This is the verdict form. Upon making your decision, please fill out the form, sign and date it, and then return with your verdict to the courtroom.

U.S. DISTRICT COURT
FOR THE STATE OF NITA
Civil Division

SHARON WATSON,	)	
	)	
Plaintiff,	)	CAL: 2011-CIV-10886
v.	)	
	)	
CENTURY TECHNOLOGIES, INC.,	)	
	)	
Defendant.	)	

We, the Jury, return the following verdict, and each of us concurs in the verdict:

[Choose the appropriate verdict]

We, the Jury, unanimously find as follows in response to the questions submitted to us:

Question 1

Did Defendant Century Technologies, Inc. discriminate on the basis of age when it terminated Plaintiff Watson?

    YES _____   NO _____

If your answer to this question is YES, please go to the next question. If your answer to this question is NO, please go to the end of the verdict form and sign and date where indicated.

Question 2

What is the amount of Plaintiff's damages?

    $ _____

_____

Date

_____

Foreperson